MAITREYA
and the
STRUGGLE AGAINST GLOBAL POVERTY

Jack Schauer

Copyright © 2023 **Jack Schauer Publishing, Inc**

All rights reserved. No part of this publication may be reproduced, distributed, or transmitted in any form or by any means, including photocopying, recording, or other electronic or mechanical methods, without the prior written permission of the publisher, except in the case of brief quotations embodied in critical reviews and certain other noncommercial uses permitted by copyright law. For permission requests, write to the publisher, addressed "Attention: Book Rights and Permission," at the address below.

Published in the United States of America

ISBN 978-1-958518-34-2 (SC)
ISBN 978-1-958518-99-1 (HC)
ISBN 978-1-958518-35-9 (Ebook)

Jack Schauer Publishing, Inc
201 11th St N
#201 Fargo, ND 58102, USA
www.stellarliterary.com

Ordering Information and Rights Permission:

Quantity sales. Special discounts might be available on quantity purchases by corporations, associations, and others. For details, contact the publisher at the address above.

For Book Rights Adaptation and other Rights Permission. Call us at toll-free 1-888-945-8513 or send us an email at admin@stellarliteray.com.

Table of Contents

Foreword iv
Introduction viii
   I - Maitreya and World Poverty 1
   II - U.S. and European Marshall Plan 4
   III - Problem of Third World Poverty 8
   IV - Lodge and Wilson 11
   V - Maitreya's Vision for the Future 14
   VI - The United Nations, the United States, and the European Union ... 18
   VII - The United Nations Millennium Development Goals 22
   VIII - Global Measurements of Poverty 27
   IX - Corporate Social Responsibility 33
   X - The Case of the European Union 38
   XI - Innovation in Organization and Leadership 41
   XII - Investment in Human and Social Capital 52
   XIII - An International Code of Ethics 56
   XIV - Social Business 60
   XV - Capitalist versus Democratic Socialist Economy 63
   XVI - Political Ethics and the International Order 66
   XVII - Conclusion 69
References 72
   Endnotes 80

Foreword

As a doctoral student in international relations at Argosy University, Sarasota campus, I began to focus upon the ability of MNCs (multinational corporations) in providing aid to lesser developed nations and/or populations mostly located within the Third World. I began this journey or quest, if you wish, some eight or nine years earlier when a friend suggested I read a book about the spiritual teacher Maitreya, and it made a great impact upon me personally. The philosophical notion I adhere to as indicated by Maitreya is ultimate liberty or "autonomy" for the individual, and thus, free will or free choice is the ethos that is demanded in recognition of these ideas.

In a sense, it was to be an in-depth analysis of corporate America in terms of addressing the need for investments in social awareness and social welfare. This was also a notion that emphasized the huge importance and need for "right relationships" among all members of humanity but particularly among nongovernmental organizations (NGOs), MNCs, international aid agencies, local governments subsisting in poverty, the World Bank and the International Monetary Fund (IMF), the United Nations (UN), and, as Lodge and Wilson portray, the creation of a World Development Corporation. (More of what this all implies will be focused upon later.) In addition, it implies what Fr. Richard Rohr calls collective consciousness, which exemplifies the "third eye" and is powerful, much more powerful, than individual consciousness as this in turn exemplifies the totality of thoughts and beliefs of a group and/or team of people.

As I was raised as a Roman Catholic, the church's social justice teachings influenced me a great deal (e.g., compassion for the poor and sick) in terms of how this eventually led me to grasp the teachings of Maitreya since his basic philosophy on life mirrors almost exactly the social gospel and teachings of the Catholic Church, although there were parts of Catholic ideology that this author still questioned (Fr. Richard Rohr's criticism of New Age ideology in terms of its lack of accountability). On the other hand, the beliefs and predictions of Maitreya (considered a world teacher) made a great deal of sense in terms of working toward a spiritual level of perfection here on Earth. This in turn enhanced my solid beliefs that reincarnation (i.e., a series of past lifetimes) was a valid and more meaningful religious philosophy than the belief in just one lifetime. The notion of just a single lifetime ran counter to my intuitive beliefs, and reincarnation gave me a greater sense of self-worth and self-esteem than that of any Western religious philosophy. It gave me a greater perspective on the need for justice in terms of integral humanity. Although the notion of reincarnation runs contrary to the teachings or philosophy of the Catholic Church, I nevertheless believe that the Catholic Church and the world teacher Maitreya have a great deal more in common than the doctrinal issues that might divide them, perhaps even more so the ideas and teaching of theosophy that symbolize the teachings of Maitreya to a much greater extent than Catholicism, particularly the notion or theosophical doctrine of individual "service." However, service is an important component of Catholicism as well as its social justice message.

According to Crème, in paraphrasing the teacher Maitreya, one of the main issues that holds human beings from advancing to a higher spiritual state or, more precisely, initiation is the notion of glamour. This can also remain a problem for successful CEOs of global MNCs. Glamour is a focus upon the emotional state of ego and thus, in turn, living within a sense of illusion, which is similar to idealism, and also an emphasis upon fulfilling what one's ego focuses upon. Glamour itself feeds upon those things that feed the ego and makes us feel better about ourselves, even if it be only a sense of illusion, advancing or emphasizing upon one's career and accompanying sense of rationalism focused upon success, success, and even more success and overall concern only for one's personal sense of happiness and fulfillment, disregarding others' happiness as not worthy of one's own personal ends or ego. It really fuels the sense of narcissism of the baby-boomer generation, especially, such as the "me generation" of the 1970s. Glamour is perhaps the most important reason keeping humanity from reaching the initiation process or holding us back from a sense of spiritual satisfaction. This also appears to Richard Rohr's emphasis upon descent rather than ascent.

One main influence regarding the doctrine or religion of Catholicism was the writings of Thomas Merton. Paraphrasing Fr. Richard Rohr, who was also heavily influenced by Merton, in Merton's book *Conjectures of a Guilty Bystander*, he writes of a mystical experience one day while standing on a busy street corner in Louisville, Kentucky. Merton suddenly realized in watching the various crowds of individuals walking to and fro and across the street how deeply he loved all these people and that he felt a sense of oneness with all humanity. Thus, he was able to transcend his false egotistic self and come to the full realization concerning God's love connection with all humanity as well as all humanity's innate love connections with one another. These statements underscore what Maitreya is attempting to bring about in terms of his notion that the wealthiest of people should share their resources with the poorest of people within this world and that that kind of compassionate love is what is truly needed to overcome the sense of evil and global displacement that rules most of our world today (and has always ruled humanity, unfortunately). It is spiritual ideals such as these that, this author believes, are necessary to promote the type of mutual understanding that most of humanity has not yet achieved. Whenever it is achieved, I think the "reappearance" phenomenon concerning Maitreya will take place. The reappearance of Maitreya will occur when he feels that humanity is sufficiently open to a doctrine that I labeled the "Doctrine of Spiritual Inevitability" but that really implies such beliefs of feeding the starving masses, particularly, which Maitreya feels will go a long way toward healing the problems inherent in the twenty-first century.

Thus, by the time that I began my doctoral program in business administration at Argosy University, I had already immersed myself in the writings and/or beliefs of Maitreya and thus, in turn, what the implications of those very same writings were for the global population. In addition, I began focusing upon the belief of the sharing of resources in terms of the MNC as well as those global institutions that were set up after World War II to try and help lesser developed nations, particularly in the Third World, institutions such as the World Bank, the IMF, the global NPOs, (nonprofit organizations) as well as the UN and its Millennium Development Goals (i.e., 2025) to end global poverty as we know it today. In addition, it is important to note that the global economic system is broken in terms of who is controlling global trade and that the international monetary system and the World Bank, under the control of the United States and a few other global trade partners, are still rather limited in scope in terms of helping those populations who are poverty stricken in the Third World. I believe that this system of affairs (e.g., IMF and the World Bank) needs to change and/or undergo a reformation for poverty on a global level to begin to be effectively dealt with.

Introduction

During the mid-to latter eighties, I completed a master's degree in the liberal arts at Moorhead State University (1987). The title of that master's thesis was "Profiles in Political Compassion." This was perhaps my first real attempt to explore the concept of compassion (e.g., compassionate leaders) in politics and public policy. This really served as the basis or foundation from which I began to further explore the notion of true compassionate leadership and laid the way (if you can call it that) for further spiritual investigation into the concept of Maitreya and his economic and/or political platform (e.g., as a world teacher).

Two of the three individuals I had chosen for that thesis, Robert Kennedy and Jane Addams, were especially similar in that they were both highly sensitive and compassionate individuals who had undergone character transformation but who were also committed to specific intellectual or political ideologies. Michael Harrington, on the other hand, was primarily an intellectual writer whose political philosophy of democratic socialism exemplified the kind of pragmatic, compassionate concerns of Kennedy and Addams. These three individuals also exemplified a commitment to a political compassion that sought to administer to the whole of society in attempting to foster a sense of harmony among the various social classes in America. In addition, these three individuals exemplified an emotional commitment to the cause of the poor and dispossessed.

What inspired Jane Addams to begin Hull House in 1889? According to her autobiography, *Twenty Years at Hull-House*, Jane Addams relates that after college, she became quite depressed, and although she traveled frequently and took various rest cures, she was unable to shake her despondency. Then while visiting London, she happened across an East London street where a large mass of humanity had huddled together for something to eat. This vision of starving people became a recurring obsession to her, and it is highly probable that this experience prompted Jane Addams to consider the idea of beginning a settlement house in America. It would seem to me that Addams, through her own pain and suffering, identified with these East London people who were starving and that it was probably this psychological catalyst that motivated Adams to want to do something about the problems of poverty.

According to Jane Addams in her autobiography, Hull House was opened on the theory "that the dependence of classes on each other is reciprocal and that as the social relation is a reciprocal relation, it gives a form of expression that has peculiar value" (Addams, p. 76). For Jane Addams, Christianity as expressed in the religious truth of Jesus was the same as the political equivalent of interpreting democracy in social terms. What Addams was attempting to realize was the idea that just as the settlement movement was embodied within society itself and not just within a certain sect, so too would Christianity, through the teaching of Jesus, serve the function of bringing different social classes of people closer together.

Today, living within these postmodernist times, one wonders if it might not be beyond that test of individuals to accomplish justice and equality for all people, not just within our own country but also as well throughout the world. For example, Michael Harrington, in his book *The Accidental Century* (which I feel has particular relevance even today), states that concentrated corporate power, through its selfish misuse of technology, blundered into a new social revolution without even having an awareness about it. What Harrington meant is that corporate businessmen and technologists, in following their own individual and collectivist aims, accidentally transformed human society—and often in a negative manner. As a result, according to Harrington, the "accidental revolution" occurred not from this or that loss of faith "but in introducing doubt and contradiction into every

Western creed, secular or religious." (Harrington, p. 36). In addition, as Harrington wrote, "Western man revolutionized everything except himself" (Harrington, p. 146).

The result of this was decadence or the idea that man had outstripped his own vision of himself in creating a new reality of human life. According to Harrington, the unique characteristic of this decadence is that a kind of loss of faith occurred in which humanity no longer believed in anything or anyone. In addition, as Max Weber formulated it, the modern world was characterized by an increase in functional reality—that is, scientific principles—while substantive reality, which saw life as a meaningful experience, began declining. "The fate of our time," wrote Weber, "is characterized by rationalization and intellectualism and, above all, by the disenchantment of the world" (Harrington, p. 165). It is this crisis of belief and disbelief, states Harrington, that is at the source of man's alienation and loss of faith in society. He writes, "The problem of both religion and atheistic humanism is the same: that a puzzled society without hunger or freedom has no need for any higher values of any kind" (Harrington, p. 175). This exemplifies postmodernist thinking at its very roots.

In his book *The Coming of the Post-Industrial Society*, Daniel Bell writes that although a postindustrial society cannot provide any sense of a transcendent ethic, the lack of a transcendent ethic or deeply rooted moral system is the deepest challenge to its survival. For example, in Berger, Berger, and Kellner's book, *The Homeless Mind*, the authors point out that throughout history, most individuals lived in life worlds (everyday realities of various human groups) that were basically unified. Today, however, modern life is highly segmented, and so the average individual inevitably comes in contact with many different kinds of life worlds. The technological and public spheres of modern living are two spheres that are highly segmented. The result of this pluralization of life worlds can result in a feeling of fear and alienation. Daniel Bell's solution that some type of transcendent ethics is necessary to sustain individuals in modern times seems to me an appropriate response.

I believe that Wendell Berry would agree with Albert Camus, who felt that though this world may have no meaning, there is something in it that does, and that is man. Therefore, if human life is to have paramount value, it is necessary to nurture and preserve this value so that individuals may have the necessary strength of dignity and integrity to confront the absurdity of the modern technological world and its accidental character. Kennedy, Addams, and Harrington, in my view, all focus upon the innate goodness of humanity rather than the evil within the world in developing their own sense of political compassion. Although postmodernist thought begins with the "decentered" individual, an emphasis upon the illusion of ego, once the veil of ego is suppressed, the true personality of the individual shines through.

In the sense that political compassion is a virtue, Robert Kennedy reminds me of Jane Addams in his sense of basic moral obligation. One clear example of this was Kennedy's program of slum regeneration in New York's Bedford–Stuyvesant District. Kennedy's plan was to get private enterprise involved in the setting up of several community corporations that would be run by the residents of Bedford–Stuyvesant themselves. In return, those private businesses who had invested the capital would receive tax incentives and low-cost loans to make it economically feasible. Like Addams, Kennedy saw that for this project to become successful, the whole community must become involved. "An effort in one problem area," Kennedy stated when the project began, "was almost worthless" (Newfield, p. 99). As Kennedy asserted, a program for housing without simultaneous programs for jobs, education, welfare reform, health, and economic development could not succeed.

In essence, Kennedy's Bedford–Stuyvesant project sought to employ people in planning and building their own communities. As James Ridgeway, in the January 1967 issue of the *New Republic*, wrote, "His program allows for and encourages local diversity; it is meant to place control with the people . . . Work, not just income, is what determines one's sense of self-importance in the country . . . the Kennedy plan aims to put people to work" (Newfield, p. 101).

Michael Harrington professes the kind of compassion in politics that Robert Kennedy and Jane Addams exemplified. Harrington's philosophy of democratic socialism is, in reality, an attempt to redress the injustice of the poorest groups trapped at the bottom of society. Harrington's vision of political compassion is the vision of a nation and a world in which every child born has a decent opportunity for education, medical care, and employment. Harrington, like Kennedy and Addams, focuses upon the welfare of society as a whole; he attempts to redress the moral concerns of all the various social classes in America.

Harrington further believes that for Western man to save himself, the accidental revolution must be made conscious and democratic. He also believes that for technology to be directed humanely, it must be placed under social democratic control. In addressing corporate collectivization of power not only in America but as well on a global level, Harrington believes that corporate businessmen have been destroying capitalist motivation, ideology, and personality through freeing themselves from the law of supply and demand. He feels that the large corporate powers on a global level are corrupting not only themselves but the future of society as well.

Harrington believes that because the way in which men produce their worldly goods is becoming more and more social, people in the West can freely and democratically take control of their lives and their destiny (e.g., through freedom of will and free choice). Harrington cites nationalization of industry as one technique that would abolish the political and social power that results from concentrated private ownership. Two other ways to achieve greater public power, according to Harrington, are through monetary and fiscal policy. Education and health care are several other important areas, Harrington believes, that could be greatly improved through national planning. In essence, what Harrington is calling for is democratic planning for work and leisure, an increasingly social allocation of resources, and a practical attack on the power of money in all its forms.

Another philosophical genius, Friedrich Nietzsche, perhaps the foremost psychologist of the twentieth century, wrote of the essence of his notion of "willpower," which, for him, symbolized man's obsession with attaining power. He believes that this is the main catalyst of change in humanity for the twentieth century in particular; in fact, this author also believes that Nietzsche's superman is not a hybrid individual as exemplary of the Germanic race (as Hitler believed) but an individual who sought power for the good of man and that that same individual exemplified not only a strict honesty of mind but also sincerity of spirit and later detachment of body/mind. However, Nietzsche did not believe that humanity would accomplish this necessarily in one lifetime but over a period of recurrent lifetimes. This notion of recurrent lifetimes and/or human nature underscores Maitreya's notion of individual human beings living many lifetimes to achieve the status of a higher spiritual entity or master.

I believe that Nietzsche came closest in his beliefs and writing to Maitreya's vision for man attaining honesty of mind, sincerity of spirit, and detachment from body. Ironically, it was Nietzsche's essay(s) on the individual psychology of attainment of power that also came to exemplify Maitreya's discussion of humanity's need to overcome his or her need for absolute power, no matter how justified. In essence, Nietzsche laid the philosophical foundation of power for twentieth-century man, in which he believed that God truly was "dead" in the minds of his contemporaries, but that in itself did not imply that man was "permitted" to do anything and everything he might wish to do. In addition, two world wars, mass genocide, and the creation of the first atomic bomb not only signaled that Nietzsche was on the right track but also, in the aftermath of World War II, inevitably led to the early reappearance of Maitreya in the Asian section of London. In essence, two separate souls: one of Nietzsche and an honest inclination of emotion and power; and the other of Maitreya, a lack of emotion and power that exemplified his philosophy of the various steps to attain in striving to become a master. While both men differed in personality and intention, still, I believe that they both came to exemplify the notions of honesty, sincerity, and detachment. Nietzsche perhaps did not attain master status, but his philosophy of the human mind and body not only underscored but also, I would argue, inevitably led from a historical, political, and social set of perspectives to the reappearance of Maitreya. Thus, I would state that the Maitreyan project was a culmination of differences between modernist and postmodernist thought in which Nietzsche, as a twentieth-century philosopher, came closest to exemplify. In other words, Nietzsche prepared the way for postmodernist and Wilbur's tier two thinking.

In terms of Ken Wilbur's notion of second-tier thinking—relating to a four-quadrant division of political thought since the Age of Enlightenment, when both liberalism and scientism arose as a paradigmatic process—Wilbur emphasizes that both liberalism and conservativism are both equally important to the process of transcendence from first tier into second tier. For example, liberalism, which focuses upon exterior forces, lacks the interior values and/or forces that conservatism implies. In addition, conservatism, which focuses upon interior values, lacks the important forces of liberalism. Both philosophies are, in and of themselves, lacking a sense of the whole and need to be able to come together; or else, neither philosophy will suffice to be able to transcend unto the second tier.

For example, Wilbur points out that traditional conservative thought is "rooted in a conventional, mythic membership, sociocentric wave of development (Wilbur, p. 85). Wilbur states that the most important consideration toward an integral politics united the best of both liberal and conservative viewpoints. Liberal exterior factors include "economic conditions, material well-being, technological advance, social safety net, and environment" (Wilbur, p. 84). On the other hand, the values of conservatism "tend to be grounded in a mythic religious orientation (the Bible)," usually focusing upon "family values and patriotism" (p. 85).

I

Maitreya and World Poverty

Perhaps it is time to put down on paper my personal quest (in a sense, my overall passion) for the future, my own struggle against poverty, whether on an individual basis or of suffering humanity as a whole. I am attempting to write a book on the topic of how to end poverty, especially in the Third World and/or on a global level. Currently, even the United States is woefully underfunding aid for the underdeveloped countries of the Third World. During the George Bush Jr. presidency, while the United States agreed to fund an amount equivalent to (1 or 2 percent of the total federal budget) barely seven billion dollars a year, the funds needed on a yearly basis to make a difference in ending poverty comes to well over a hundred billion dollars.

To begin with, I must confess that I have a specific viewpoint or set of perspectives of which I feel it is important to examine. Every two thousand years, our earthly civilization undergoes another paradigm of change. According to Benjamin Crème, we (i.e., humanity) have been under the impact of the powerful cosmic energies of Pisces. Presently, after two thousand years, we have entered a new millennium based upon the cosmic energies of Aquarius.

Having just passed into this new cycle, as Crème points out, there will inevitably be mass spiritual changes in the way human beings interact with one another; individuals will become much more interested in their personal growth and thus, in turn, make achieving spiritual perfection as the ultimate goal of each lifetime. In essence, we are undergoing a massive spiritual crisis that, according to Crème, can only be resolved by truly addressing our economic and political problems (on a global scale), and this, in turn, implies that these same problems are actually a spiritual crisis, based upon our human notion of "separatism." This sense of separatism, as Crème points out, is, in reality, an illusion; this illusion can only be resolved through energies of freedom and justice, and this, in turn, can only come about through an emphasis upon sharing. All earthly resources need to be shared and balanced so that the starving masses can be saved and the richest individuals in the world will come to a spiritual realization that this is the only way that they can truly save themselves. In terms of right relationships, complacency appears to be the real evil with which to confront.

This brings us to a discussion of the world teacher Maitreya. He is the most highly spiritualized person on Earth (seventh-level initiate); he overshadowed both Buddha and Jesus Christ (for the last three years of his life as teacher and founder of Christianity). He had been living in the highest reaches of the Himalayas but returned to take up residence in London in 1977 as he felt the spiritual energies surrounding the earth were making it more and more likely that his mission and vision for the world would be accepted by a global audience.

According to Crème, Maitreya and his masters have come to teach humanity how to live correctly, "as brothers and sisters of one humanity, creating therefore freedom for all, justice for all, and peace for everyone" (Crème, p. 9). According to Maitreya, he has come to teach "self-realization" or "God-realization" to humanity. For individuals to attain self-realization, they must seek to attain "honesty of mind, sincerity of spirit, and detachment of body" (pp. 9–11).

Maitreya's philosophical essence is the law of karma, which is regulated by the doctrine of cause and effect. All life beings, human beings, have a choice of free will, and since Maitreya won't interfere with the free will of human beings, it comes down to abiding by the law of cause and effect. As such, many individuals (i.e., the whole of humanity) must understand that if something evil or negative befalls their life—wars or even negative climate change—Maitreya won't interfere because if he did, he would be violating the essence of cause and effect (i.e., free will). Thus, he has come primarily to show humanity how to save itself. However, he has written, that doesn't imply that he won't be working behind the scenes in a multitude of ways.

However, one aspect of all this, global warming, which can have the most negative impact upon the planet, will only be successfully dealt with by the intervention of Maitreya. If one accepts the notion of the "doomsday effect"—that is, runaway global warming—we could be looking at a scenario with climate change three to five degrees, and this could ultimately lead to extinction. However, not only will we need to reverse the effects of global warming, but also, part of the solution will ultimately come through the sharing of resources between the haves and the have-nots of the world. Thus, in turn, both economic and political solutions will be just as important to the ecological maintenance of our planet as solutions of an ecological nature. All three of these kinds of solutions need to be pragmatically assessed to achieve an end to global warming. In turn, the energy crisis is another crisis like global poverty that will need to be addressed by humanity within the short term.

II

U.S. and European Marshall Plan

It seems to this writer that the most practical manner or the surest way to end poverty would be for the United States and the European Union (EU) to develop another Marshall Plan, when the United States put together an aid plan of money and food that focused on helping feed and clothe the refugees in post–World War II Germany. This type of scenario or action(s) would result in the quickest method of putting to an end poverty and starvation among the people of the Third World in particular and the entire world in general.

One of the main problems in terms of ending worldwide poverty and hunger has to do with Robert Gitlin's notion of "industrial organization," which implies that since more-profitable MNCs achieve higher economies of scale, less-profitable MNCs are often driven out of the market since they are unable to compete effectively against these larger MNCs or oligarchies. This is the concept of industrial organization as it relates to the theory of international trade and endogenous growth.

Gitlin utilizes the theory of both "industrial organization" and "endogenous growth" to explain the current models of globalism and those MNCs that will be most successful. According to the new theories of economic thinking, since neoclassical economics does not recognize history and geography in explaining economic affairs, according to Gilpin (2001), it also cannot explain the growth process and its effects on the power and interests of major actors. Thus, it is hardly possible to understand the dynamics of the world economy. In addition, since neoclassical theory does not consider the importance of technological innovation as it relates to the importance of imperfect or oligopolistic competition, neoclassical economics alone cannot explain present-day global economics. In effect, endogenous growth theory "suggests that government policies, through promotion of an increased national savings and investment rate . . . [and] increased support for research and development, can lead to a sustained higher rate of economic growth" (p. 113).

According to this author, the implications of endogenous theory leading to industrial organization (increasing returns to scale, e.g., oligarchic organizations) cannot necessarily lead to a state of affairs where richer nations will want to invest resources in lesser developed nations or economies. Thus, in terms of organizations leading to increasing returns to scale—with greater investment(s) in human capital, research, development, and technological innovation—this, in turn, has the general effect of making rich nations richer and poor nations even poorer. This entails a paradigm shift in which way global trade is carried among the most powerful multinational organizations and impacting other organizations such as the International Monetary Fund and the World Bank.

Although Maitreya endorses a decentralized spirit of globalism and thus endorses global localism or even regionalism to a certain degree, he also believes this for pragmatic reasons and not for reasons of social Darwinist, cutthroat capitalism. He believes that political and social enhancement from a spiritual perspective will work best or be best enhanced from a decentralized or regionalized sense of globalism; he feels that politics and social behavior work best when the people themselves decide on a local, state, or regional level what problems need to be solved and what solutions will work best to address these same problems. But really, it is Ken Wilbur's notion of integralism that brings together all the various facets (religious, economic, business, political, etc.) of humankind integrated in a holistic kind of order. This, in turn, relates to Wilbur's notion of "a theory of everything."

According to Muller and Stoger (2009), a global Marshall Plan such as the one in which the United States was primarily engaged in post–

World War II Germany is a long-term plan for a just world, possibly based on the European model but perhaps best described as an "ecosocial market economy." The millennium goals of the UN, according to these authors, are described as existing within an intermediary step; in fact, all the nations of the world have already reached agreement on these goals (ending poverty now by 2025). However, the main problem is that funds are limited, and the priorities of rich nations like the United States are different (e.g., homeland security threats). In addition, according to Muller and Stoger, in paraphrasing Professor Radermacher, all the nations of the world and the international organizations, such as the World Trade Organization (WTO) and the IMF, have also reached an agreement on these goals.

In his book *The End of Poverty* (2008) Sachs, director of the UN Millennium Project, believes that the extreme poor are trapped within a cycle of poverty by disease, physical isolation, climate stress, and environmental degradation, and thus, external or foreign assistance should be in the form of debt-free (i.e. usury, noninterest) aid. This will also help jumpstart the economic process of capital accumulation within the Third World countries, which will then lead to rising incomes. Sachs writes that we ought to create a global fund for smallholder food production (production on farms of two hectares or less) in the same manner that we have a global fund for AIDS, tuberculosis, and malaria. Sachs believes that this will produce a tremendous result at a low cost and would avoid a great deal of suffering and famine and a lot of the need for much more expensive food aid.

Hoffberg (2006) takes issue with Sachs's belief that the extreme poor are trapped within a cycle of poverty, whether through disease, physical isolation, climate stress, or environmental degradation. A different take on moral obligations and ethical thought with respect to international politics, Young (as cited in Hutchings, 2004, p. 241) argues for a feminist ethics that is specifically concerned with international, transnational, or global political contexts and issues. This type of discourse development is also labeled in various ways, including communicative ethics or dialogue ethics, according to

Young. Rather than focusing upon the field of ethical inquiry as a Christian responsibility (e.g., peace and justice), Young consistently argues for and stresses the importance of actual dialogue and the need to allow for a multiplicity of ways of articulating and communicating ideas and interests, whether from a sense of moral justice or some other ethical perspective.

Hutchings's (2004) article dealing with "feminist ethics" as it relates to the international community is concerned with the feminist dilemma between moral universalism and moral pluralism, which she feels is specifically concerned with international or political issues on a global level. Hutchings argues in favor of the "civil society" ethical argument, which appears to work on a more multicultural level. She also cites Benhabib's argument that the conditions for ethical inquiry on a global level or setting should include "universal respect" and "egalitarian reciprocity" (p. 243).

The most recent "Global Plan Initiative" was propounded by Al Gore back in 1990. Although Gore is most often associated with the modern ecology movement, ecology is closely linked with the problems of poverty and starvation; as it appears that both problematic areas, are interchangeable in terms of improvement and/or developing greater levels of sustainability. It is estimated that one of the results of the Global Marshall plan is that, in terms of economic development and greater sustainability it "will boost the human potential of three billion people." (External Link: Global Marshall Plan Initiative).

III

Problem of Third World Poverty

One of the purposes of this research is to examine the problem of Third World poverty in terms of the modern MNC and how the MNC of today can perform its economic and political mission while at the same time pursue issues of a humanitarian or social-justice nature. It is this writer's belief that the problem(s) of Third World poverty (particularly extreme poverty) must be confronted by the MNC of today in terms of the struggle by the UN, which has called the problem of global poverty "the preeminent moral and humanitarian challenge of our age" (Lodge, 2002, p. 12).

Lodge and Wilson (2006) also state that the modern MNC and its managers are hamstrung by a lack of legitimacy in the sense that everyone, from the CEOs and down the corporate ladder, can't respond effectively to the challenges of Third World poverty (and other extreme areas of poverty around the globe) because their response requires them to cooperate with people (e.g., the community) who don't trust their intentions. This is particularly true of capitalist economies versus economies of a democratic socialist nature.

The global community, broadly speaking, is no longer satisfied that managers and their corporations are fully law-abiding as they go about increasing shareholder value. Communities want more from global businesses, but they don't trust managers to provide "more" because they haven't in the past. Thus, the cycle of distrust regarding global corporations continues, while at the same time, demands and expectations rise in the face of declining legitimacy (Lodge & Wilson,

2006). Again, this raises the issue of whether or not capitalist economies can realistically confront extreme poverty on a global level or the belief that economies of a democratic socialist nature (this also implies government planning) are the only realistic ones to challenge extreme poverty. I will examine this in more detail in a later chapter. These beliefs need to be further analyzed from a political and economic perspective(s). According to Lodge and Wilson (2006), as mankind evolves, the changing nature of MNCs is also becoming much more responsive to poverty in the Third World nations. In addition, a whole field of endeavor dedicated to CSR (corporate social responsibility) has already taken root within most global organizations today in the twenty-first century, and it is here to stay, continuing to evolve into more pragmatic moral and spiritual duties expected within the global MNC and the partnerships it engages in.

For example, according to Lodge and Wilson (2006), there is much greater faith in the notion of local partnerships among large numbers of NGOs "or local branches of international NGOs" working "at the country level with MNCs in developing countries" (Lodge & Wilson, 2006, p. 61). One way for MNCs to gain legitimacy within the developing world is this type of partnership with NGOs in which there is a combination of objectives by both MNCs and NGOs and in which MNCs are becoming much socially responsive, stressing "social and community objectives," while, on the other hand, NGOs are seeking greater "revenue streams and profit sources to help insure their sustainability and effectiveness" (Lodge & Wilson, p. 61).

In an interview with Charlie Rose, former president Clinton cited that today, on a global level, there is a political, economic, and social crisis occurring. In addition, he states that there are literally millions of refugees throughout the world; Clinton talked about his own foundation that is doing its best to make a huge contribution globally in terms of AIDS, drugs, antipoverty, and financial investments throughout the Third World in particular. The Clinton Foundation is a great example of funding those extreme underdeveloped countries throughout the Third World in its mission to lessen the impact of these global problems in terms of an economic, social, and political/international nature or context. However, the main obstacle to raising the necessary foreign aid assistance has to do with individuals as a whole. There is neither the willpower nor compassion for the richest 10 percent of the global economy to make these kinds of foreign aid investments. It boils down to simple greed; unfortunately, that is the bottom line in terms of the richest 10 percent to try and provide not only foreign assistance to those in the Third World but also poverty assistance throughout the entire world. This is where the mission and vision of the world teacher Maitreya has made a commitment to humanity to end worldwide poverty.

Former president Clinton, in his interview with Charlie Rose (September 2016), stated that the global economy still has not fully recovered from the worldwide recession of 2008. In Clinton's (2006) address to the General Assembly of the United Nations, he portrayed the United States and the EU as sharing a common vision of a market-based global economy. President Clinton still maintains his faith in a capitalistic set of market forces to help underdeveloped nations across the globe. Through a mutual commitment, the Transatlantic Economic Partnership (TEP), the EU, with the support of the United States, can promote and together stress the importance of good governance and respect for human rights, including core labor standards and more effective investment in education, training, and efficient and transparent institutions.

The Mutual Recognition Agreement, signed in 1998, is a good example of the United States and the EU struggling against the perils associated with global poverty by supporting a fuller participation of the developing countries in the WTO and in future multilateral trade negotiations, with the emphasis upon better integration of these same nations in the world economic system (Clinton, 2006). However, this author questions whether any capitalistic global market economy (or economies) can pragmatically make a set of positive advancements in trying to solve the questions of poverty and hunger not only in the Third World but on a global perspective as well. Capitalism may need to give way to democratic socialism, according to many scholars, if there is to be a successful future struggle against global poverty.

IV

Lodge and Wilson

In an attempt to identify arguments stronger than social justice, ways to justify social welfare need to be identified that are consistent with the international market economy and the importance of its application to various countries and societies (Lodge, 2002). Since social welfare has almost always been viewed from the standpoint of consumption and distribution, the connection with production has hardly ever been explored. In turn, the five benefits—including human capital, social benefits, societal morale and cohesion, economic benefits, and civility and aesthetics—should not be identified as arguments against social justice but should be viewed as an effort to supplant arguments of a social and humanitarian nature (Lodge, 2002).

In addition, Lodge (2002) argues that global political, economic, and social stability, whether Western or not, depends upon world governments to maintain a certain sense of "legitimacy," which also implies broadening the political and social involvement including the poor (Lodge, 2002). According to Lodge, while many governments and their leaders believe that globalization is the modern "cure-all," it will not eradicate world poverty by itself. The survival of the world's poor, as Lodge points out, implies that the survival of global corporations is both directly and indirectly tied to solving these problems (p. 6).

Although world leaders have given the reduction of global poverty a top priority (e.g., the Millennium Development Goals of the UN), Lodge and Wilson (2006) state that poverty still persists on a deeper level. In addition, as these authors state, in many countries where poverty has worsened, governments lack either the desire or ability to act; they argue, however, that the solution lies in the creation of a new institution, "the World Development Corporation" (WDC), a partnership of MNCs, international development agencies, and NGOs committed to the eradication of extreme poverty. If the world's leaders, in union with the UN, could be convinced that not only will global terrorism be defeated but global poverty as well, they may come together as has just been outlined in terms of MNCs.

Lodge and Wilson (2006) believe that MNCs have the critical combination of capabilities (human capital, investment income, organizational and productive capacity, etc.) that are required to build investment, grow economies, and create jobs in poor countries and thus to reduce poverty. To reiterate what was discussed in the previous paragraph, these same authors believe that MNCs can reduce poverty and do it profitably and also from a perspective of sustainability. However, they also point out, as has already been discussed, that today's MNCs lack legitimacy within these underdeveloped countries of the Third World and across the globe. Thus, they believe that a collective approach is better than one in which an individual corporation proceeds alone. Thus, it is the authors' view that a UN-sponsored World Development Corporation, owned and managed by a dozen or so MNCs with NGO support, will make a much greater difference.

According to Lodge and Wilson (2006), what is presently occurring on a global scale is that not only are the world's MNCs being increasingly questioned in terms of "legitimacy," but also, the old ideas that managers still cling to in terms of their authority are insufficient "to meet global expectations" (p. 162). According to these authors, the corporation, as "the principal driver of globalization, is now expected to pay greater heed to the needs of the communities that it affects, among which is the alleviation of poverty in much of the world" (p. 162).

Lodge and Wilson believe that the creation of a World Development Corporation would "equip the corporation with the legitimacy that can be bestowed by the UN, NGOs, and the communities it affects and also to provide it with sufficient public resources to enable it to serve community needs—that is, reduce poverty without threatening its survival as a profit-making institution" (p. 163).

In addition, Lodge and Wilson (2006) cite Sachs (2005), who states that organizations such as the World Bank, Freedom House, Transparency International, and a growing list of African countries have the quality of leadership and governance to achieve economic development, but they lack the means. These same authors point out that in developing countries, there is a desperate need for infrastructure, roads, electricity, health care, and education. They argue that this is where the World Development Corporation would create positive benefits in reducing poverty, particularly in those regions of the world in which poverty has been most resilient, where individual corporations are reluctant to invest alone, and in which traditional foreign assistance has been most disappointing. This type of antipoverty project would not only raise incomes in very poor countries but also heighten motivation for education, improved health as nutrition improves, and new social organization and community leadership. In turn, increased political participation (particularly of the participatory democracy type) would empower individuals to gain power over their environment and begin to realize that they can change the system around them.

Lodge and Wilson (2006) argue that if there is to be hope in terms of MNCs (with their extraordinary resources and abilities) to make a difference in lifting developing countries out of poverty, they cannot do this on their own; they will also need the help and collaboration of governmental and nongovernmental development organizations. In addition, while modern MNCs lack a sense of "legitimacy" in terms of reducing poverty in developing countries, 40 percent of their funding comes to them through such governmental organizations as the UN, the World Bank, and the International Monetary Fund. These NGOs, although supported by the MNCs themselves, in turn adhere to a global consciousness that is "rooted in moral convictions about rights and duties that transcend cultures and boundaries" (p. 20).

V

Maitreya's Vision for the Future

Maitreya's vision for the future involves equitable sharing of the world's resources. Without a plan that raises all individuals from poverty, there can be no justice. Without any justice, there can be no peace, and without peace, there can be no future (Maitreya, *Share International*, 2016). Maitreya goes on to state that all the essential needs of humanity—every man, woman, and child—must be met. This will involve adequate food for all human beings. His priorities include adequate housing for all people and universal health care and education. His priorities also emphasize restoration of the environment and universal peace on a global level. Stockbauer's article "The Future Role of the United Nations" portrays Maitreya's unique cultural heritage, its political and economic institutions, and its vast diversity of religious expression as inherently spiritual. An ideal future, according to Maitreya, would see the light of divinity shining equally through all humanity. In our time, Maitreya is focusing upon the political and economic fields, where he continues to inspire world leaders to implement policies that will lead to an equitable distribution of planetary resources. Maitreya teaches that the huge problem having to do with the economic and political crises that we find in the world today is fundamentally due to a sense of complacency. This sort of complacency is usually created by blind market forces, and human greed is at its epicenter. To defeat complacency and greed, Maitreya teaches that we need to fully understand the complex nature of the forces having to do with cause and effect. Once we are able to come to grips with the spiritual crisis today caused by human greed and complacency, we can then have the ability to change things for the better.

According to Maitreya, the forces of capitalism are winding down in Europe and will also wind down in the United States; a worldwide economic stock exchange crisis (the result of financial speculation) will begin in Japan (this already happened during the late 1980s) and lead to a general economic downswing or crisis throughout the world. That is the point in time when humanity will need to figure out how to feed the entire world and also come to grips with the environment. This cause-and-effect syndrome has already begun, and the inevitable result with be a breakdown of human societies across the globe. (Crème, *Share International*, 2016).

According to Lodge et at. (2002), in spite of the roughly trillion that has been spent on grants and loans to fight global poverty, since the end of World War II, nearly half the world's six billion people still live on less than $2 a day; a fifth get by on less than $1 a day. Lodge goes on to state that at times, foreign aid has even worsened the plight of the poor by sustaining the corrupt and/or inefficient governments that created the miserable conditions in the first place (Lodge et al., 2002). Not only does this call for a greater sense of responsibility for these same unfortunate and underserved populations throughout the Third World, but also, to be successful from a pragmatic perspective, the EU, along with the United States and UN, must continually strive for even newer and more innovative ways to reduce world poverty and hunger.

Leach (2009), in an interview with Devaki Jain, states that the problem of poverty is really a political question and one that cannot be solely dealt with in terms of human development questions or efforts. She believes that by not seeing the struggle against poverty in terms of political questions or issues, we are not allowing citizens to see that it's a political choice that people make on economic growth paths. She cities the "crucible test" that Gandhi gave to all Indians: that whenever life becomes too much for us, we should recall the face of the poorest and weakest man and ask ourselves if the next step we are contemplating is going to be of any use to him. Then according to Gandhi, your doubts and self will melt away.

C. Joy's (2009) interview that was printed in *Share International* was a discussion of several commonly held beliefs about hunger, poverty, and other issues of Third World development that distort and delay attempts to address human suffering. For example, Joy was asked why people in the Third World cannot grow enough food for themselves. Joy states that they "actually used to." According to her, mass hunger on the scale we see at present is a relatively new phenomenon. "In many nations, it can be traced directly back to the effects of colonialism, when nations like Britain, France, Spain, Portugal, and the Netherlands essentially invaded large parts of Asia, Africa, and Latin America so as to meet the needs of their own ideologies, countrymen, and trading partners" (Joy, *Share International*, 2010). By imposing drastic changes on the traditional cultures, they set in motion a cycle that gradually led to widespread poverty, an increased birth rate, and severe environmental damage. (Check out chapter on racism and institutionalized racism in *Politics in Compassion*.)

In addition, multinational enterprises face the challenge of operating effectively to generate knowledge across multiple boundaries (Mudambi, Mudambi & Navarra, 2007). Leadership and management are responsible for innovation and technological progress as well as knowledge production and thus must face strategic decisions on autonomy and control, working conditions, and tangible rewards (Mudambi et al., 2007). This will be extremely important for leaders and/or managers involved within the EU, the United States, and the UN in terms of fostering a sense of teamwork and a positive social environment by which organizations may display a sense of goodwill to Third World countries.

Another example of an issue that is related to globalism, especially with regard to the rise of new technologies and the aging of society and which this author believes has an indirect bearing on global poverty, is the notion of lifelong learning. Dehmel (2006) states this is a concept that the EU has promoted in terms of a policy matter. As a result of being stimulated by progress toward a single European market and by the threats as well as the opportunities afforded by globalization and new information technologies, there has been a growing interest in lifelong learning within the EU since the early 1990s (Dehmel, 2006).

Another article accessed on December 25, 2009, from the *Share International Archives* on economics states that given the unprecedented progress in human and economic development over the past fifty years, authors of a new report argue that eradicating extreme poverty in the first one or two decades of the twenty-first century is a feasible, affordable goal. But to achieve this goal, they say strategies are needed to accelerate economic growth in the one hundred countries caught in stagnation or decline, implement policies that are "propoor" or targeted at poverty reduction, and reverse the menacing setbacks that create and recreate poverty, including HIV/AIDS, violent conflict, and environmental degradation.

C. Francis (2008), in an interview for *Share International Archives,* cites historian Howard Zinn, who stated that every person on Earth should have a basic standard of living that is guaranteed, which he feels is possible since we live in a very wealthy world. According to Zinn, everyone should have fundamental human rights, including freedom of speech and freedom of the press, freedom of association, and the right to communicate with others on an equal basis so that the media are not monopolized by a small number of wealthy individuals.

To achieve this, according to Zinn, our way of thinking in the Western world (e.g., the EU and the United States) will need to change, and this could consist of a rejection of nationalism, a rejection of the idea of national borders, visas, passports, and immigration quotas. In addition, according to Zinn, the notion that the world can be divided up into a hundred or two hundred different places and reject violence and war, in stressing a spirit of world solidarity, could also create an atmosphere in which Third World poverty could be brought to an end much sooner (cited by Francis, p. 13).

VI

The United Nations, the United States, and the European Union

According to Schori (2005), it is imperative that the United States and the EU, together with the UN, become strong partners in the struggle against global poverty. Schori believes that they need to be solid partners because the world requires the United States and the EU to be politically and economically engaged in the foremost intergovernmental organization—that is, the UN. Schori goes on to state there will be no stability in the world or at the UN without the United States. Although the United States and the EU do not always agree on the means to achieve the shared vision of coming to grips with eliminating global poverty, one concrete method of improving relations across the Atlantic would be to increase contacts among parliamentarians (Schori, 2005).

The European Parliament and the different committees of national parliaments could and should develop a strategy in terms of dealing with world poverty with their counterparts in Washington (Schori, 2005). Because there is a sense of distrust, ignorance, and prejudice, cooperation on a global level is badly needed if poverty is to be reduced in the Third World. According to Schori, "unilateralism equals collateral damage, and multilateralism equals collateral benefits" (p. 277)—in essence an emphasis upon cooperation rather than intense competition.

In providing a useful scenario of how the EU, the United States, and the UN can come together in the struggle against global poverty, there are several possible roles that the UN can play in such a crucial partnership. According to *Share International* (2009), in an article by Carmen Font (2008) questioning Prof. Frederico Mayor Zaragoza, former director of UNESCO and the founder of the Foundation for the Culture of Peace as well as the World Forum on Civil Society Networks, he asserts that the UN has been gradually weakened since the Cold War despite important initiatives that have been passed along the way.

Initially, according to Zaragoza (as cited in Font, 2008), the debate within the UN was centered on how to develop all countries to the same level, whether on a political, educational, or cultural development basis. Then another notion emerged that was thought to be even more important, the "endogenous development" concept that stressed nations learning to help themselves (Font, 2008). Then the third big step in the field of economic development stressed the notion of "sustainability" (p. 3). This meant that economic development is useless if we, as citizens of the world, exhaust natural resources (p. 3). According to Zaragoza, we have not been taking any of these three basic and commonsense steps in economic development.

Font's article goes on to state the belief that to make a first step toward implementation of real development "with a human face," we need to get rid of these so-called foreign-aid loans (which are actually a form of usury) to Third World nations. According to this same article, these loans have forced cuts in the number of so-called effectives—such as teachers, doctors, nurses, social workers—and most of the money has gone to infrastructure built by donor nations since the recipients have no means to invest in training their own engineers. As a result, this approach has fostered and continues to foster a system of deeply indebted countries where the flow of aid is inverted so that recipients pay more than they receive (Font, p. 5). As a result of these loans, poor countries are financing wealthy ones (p. 5).

For the UN to play a meaningful role as a full partner with the United States and the EU in terms of the struggle against global poverty, the UN should be allowed to use more political power (Font,

2008). For example, according to Zaragoza, although the UN is neither a relief organization nor a charity, it is important for all three partners to understand that the creation of peace involves the prevention of conflict and "peacebuilding" (cited in Font, 2008). The United States, the EU, and the UN, as equal partners in the fight against global poverty, according to Font, could prevent conflict and bring an end to world poverty by creating economic conditions that would allow poor countries to gain emancipation and self-esteem.

In addition, there should be a set of guiding principles by which the United States, the EU, and the UN should abide by faithfully, according to Crème (2009), as if by the letter of the law; these ethical principles, which are part and parcel of the recognition of world poverty, particularly Third World poverty, include the following: adopting, complying, and maintaining the highest standards of business, management, and professional ethics and in dealing with relationships with benefactors, contractors, and government and civil authorities; devising and implementing systems that not only deal with specific cultures and infrastructures with regard to the United States and the EU; ensuring that the environment is respected and sustained; and ensuring those resources on a local level be optimized and managed and that opportunities be created and provided for the local population wherever possible.

To come to grips with global poverty upon a more micromanagement philosophical level, scientific experts, as a first step, need to determine a budget standard for a biological minimum that is necessary to protect a person from physical dangers to his or her life and health (Volkert, 2006). Volkert addressed the EU's conceptual shift from a narrow-income poverty perspective to a multidimensional approach. He stated that the EU used income or expenditure measures to assess poverty. However, in 2000, according to Volkert, it was decided by the member nations of the EU that two-year national action plans for combating poverty and social exclusion as well as setting specific targets should be implemented. Volkert stated that this proposal broadened the perspective from one of financial poverty to one that also included nonmonetary issues such as employment, education, housing, and health as well as such missing dimensions as political and social participation.

According to Midgeley (1993), despite the fact that World War II policymakers assumed that social security would reduce poverty significantly throughout the poverty areas of the global world, social-security programs in developing countries have had little effect in dealing with these kinds of problems. In addition, as Midgeley argues, there is a great deal of evidence that shows that social-security programs in developing countries do not reach the vast majority of those populations who are trapped within the conditions of poverty and deprivation. However, Midgeley does feel that newer innovative ways need to be explored, tested, and implemented if social security is to be an effective tool in reducing Third World poverty; one way is to examine those nations in which social security has worked.

Although this author would much prefer a political and social ideology, such as democratic socialism as the most pragmatic in terms of success, I believe that what we will need is a combination of ideologies, including capitalism, and, as well, planning in terms of democratic socialism. However true this may be, it is also true that in terms of the present forces of marketing that control the world's economies, I believe that a capitalistic vision must initially solve the problems of world hunger and poverty if for no other reason than we have no other choice in the matter. However, it is also this author's belief that by the leadership of Maitreya and his masters, capitalism can create a new Third World devoid of hunger, disease, and poverty but a type of capitalism built upon pillars of social justice.

Returning to Sachs's millennium goals, since the global end of poverty was not achieved in 2015, Sachs and the global community (United Nations) have reestablished the Millennium Development Goals for 2025. The essence of the problem was one of donor-rich nations and individuals' underfunding what was needed within the Third World to overcome Third World poverty.

VII

The United Nations Millennium Development Goals

It is this author's belief that to successfully come to grips with global poverty (particularly Third World poverty) in terms of the UN, it is also necessary that the MNC must also join the struggle, along with the World Bank, the WTO, and the IMF as well as NGOs; the more partners who support the UN Millennium Development Goals, the better the chance that those goals will be met. In terms of the MNC supporting the UN, the problem of global poverty has been called "the preeminent moral and humanitarian challenge of our age" (Lodge, 2002, p. 2). In turn, this thesis argument implies that global political stability, whether Western or not, depends upon world governments to maintain a certain sense of "legitimacy," which also implies broadening the base of political involvement to include the poor (Lodge, 2002). While many governments and their leaders believe that globalization is the modern "cure-all," it will certainly not eradicate world poverty by itself (2002). Thus, the survival of the world's poor, this author submits, implies the survival of global corporations to intervene directly to help solve these problems in support of the UN Millennium Development Goals.

Jeffrey Sachs, who is perhaps the most foremost supporter of the UN Millennium Development Goals and, in turn, a global economist trying to reach these goals, states in The End Of Poverty (2006):

the international community's approach remains incoherent in practice. On the one side, it announces bold goals, like the Millennium Development Goals and even ways that the goals can be achieved, such as the pledge of increased donor assistance made in the Monterey Consensus. Yet when it comes to real practice . . . vis-à-vis . . . in the poverty reduction plans, the millennium goals are expressed only as vague aspirations rather than operational targets . . . (pp. 270–71)

According to Sachs, while the IMF and the World Bank offer a great deal of lip service to meeting the Millennium Development Goals, they are "approving programs that will not achieve them and privately acknowledging, with business as usual, that they cannot be met" (Sachs, p. 271). Sachs argues that while the participant nation prepares a mostly realistic "poverty reduction plan," including how the aid will be dispersed, "what is missing in the process are the practical linkages between the Millennium Development Goals and the poverty reduction plans" (p. 271).

For example, as Sachs explains, in actual practice, countries are presented "with a fait accompli . . . 'here's the amount you will receive'" (p.271). Sachs goes on to explain that the process should be turned around in that the initial step "should be to learn what the country actually needs in foreign assistance. After that, the IMF and World Bank should go out to raise the required amount from the donors" (p. 271). As long as only lip service is paid to achieving the UN Millennium Development Goals, there can be no pragmatic success. What the participating donors are missing is a sense of self-will that takes the UN Millennium Development Goals seriously.

In an attempt to identify arguments stronger than social justice, ways to justify social welfare need to be identified that are consistent with the international market economy and the importance of its application to various countries and societies. Since social welfare has almost always been looked at from the standpoint of consumption and distribution, the connection with production has hardly ever been explored. In turn, the five benefits—including human capital, social benefits, societal morale and cohesion, economic benefits, and civility and aesthetics—should not be identified as arguments against social justice but should be viewed as an effort to supplant arguments of a social and humanitarian nature (Sachs, 2002).

Kenworthy (1999) argues that most social scientists, policymakers, and citizens who support the welfare state do so in part because they believe social-welfare programs help reduce the incidence of poverty. Yet according to Kenworthy, a growing number of critics assert that such programs in fact fail to decrease poverty because too small a share of transfers fails to reach the poor, because such programs create a welfare/poverty trap, or because they weaken the economy. Kenworthy's study assesses the effect of social-welfare policy extensiveness on poverty rates across fifteen affluent industrialized nations over the period 1960–91 using both absolute and relative measures of poverty; the results strongly support the conventional view that social-welfare programs reduce poverty.

Given the fact that capital market and state-planned societies are independently failures in dealing with global poverty (Third World poverty), Sachs believes that successful economies tend to be mixed economies, "relying on both the public sector and the private sector for economic development" (p. 327). Sachs states that "markets and competition alone will not provide efficient levels of infrastructure, knowledge, environmental management, and goods" (p. 327). According to Sachs, while what is true at the national level is also true at the international level, "without cooperation, a collection of national economies will not provide efficient levels of investment in cross-border infrastructure, knowledge, environmental management, or merit goods among the world's poor" (p. 327). Sachs argues that the task of eliminating poverty at the global level is a global responsibility that will have global benefits; no single nation can do it by themselves. "The hardest part is for us to think globally, but that is what global society in the twenty-first century requires" (p. 327). Thus, according to Sachs, the philosophy of the United Nations Millennium

Development Compact, which was both ratified and developed globally, can serve as the basis of these international efforts.

Craig and Porter (2005) paint a more positive picture in terms of the World Bank, the IMF, the Asian Development bank, and the UN formula of poverty reduction, which, they believe, has led to a pragmatic program appealing to the enormous organizations working in partnerships around social inclusion, development, and well-being. Craig and Porter believe that one must have a broad strategy in terms of reducing poverty, such as promoting opportunities, creating security, strengthening capabilities, and generating empowerment. According to these authors, faster growth will require policies that encourage macroeconomic stability, shift resources to more productive sectors, and integrate with the global economy. In striving for broad-based opportunities for people living in conditions of poverty and thus, in turn, rising in incomes, this should, in turn, expand opportunities and choice and provide the basis for participation in society. A society of people who enjoy high levels of participation, interconnection, and cohesion is defined in this project as possessing a high level of social capability.

On the other hand, Weber (2004) explores the relationship between the politics of Third World development and the reproduction of inequality brought about by world capitalism. Weber states that since 1945, the global politics of international development has been complicit in the making of a specific world order. Weber illustrates this by drawing on a key strategy aimed at Third World poverty and global poverty in general; this is the "Poverty Reduction Strategy Papers" (PRSP) approach, created by the World Bank and the IMF. In this qualitative study, Weber argues that the political ideology and practice of global politics reinforce the conditions of global insecurity and thus must be transcended. He seems to be stating that both the IMF and the World Bank have been coopted by world capitalism and have, in turn, stopped other more progressive alternatives having to do with democratic socialist ideals of economic development.

Anderson (2009) also argues that chronic conditions are not just a problem for industrialized countries; they also affect more than a billion people in low-and middle-income countries. This perspective shows how some middle-income countries are beginning to respond to the growing cost and prevalence of noncommunicative chronic diseases (NCDs). The primary message here, however, is that low-income countries will need substantial international assistance to confront the growing cost and burden of disease associated with NCDs. Evidence from middle-income countries, according to Anderson, suggests that there are low-cost, cost-effective ways to prevent and treat NCDs in low-income countries.

In addition to all this, Joseph Stiglitz describes in his book *Globalization and Its Discontents* (2002) that most importantly, there needs "to be a return to basic economic principles; rather than focusing on ephemeral investor psychology . . . the IMF needs to restore aggregate demand in countries facing an economic recession" (p. 240). In addition, according to Stiglitz, reassessing the goals of the World Bank suggests the importance of "living within one's budget constraints, the importance of education, including female education, and of macroeconomic stability" (p. 241).

However, other themes that Stiglitz emphasizes has also to do with "establishing a strong technological basis, which included support for advanced training . . . support for trade and openness" as well as the creation of jobs "by export expansion, not the job losses from increased imports, that gave rise to growth." (p. 241). Stiglitz states that "when governments took actions to promote exports and new enterprises, liberalization worked; otherwise, it often failed" (p. 241). "Successful countries," according to Stiglitz, "also emphasized competition over privatization and the restructuring of existing enterprises" (p. 242).

VIII

Global Measurements of Poverty

Initially, this writer was intent on examining China's rise out of poverty as a possible template for other countries (developing) in nature. In doing so, this writer spent a great amount of time examining Wong's (1995) article in Social Poverty and Administration to find the best and most just way to measure poverty. Wong's article is a qualitative study that sought to discover whether Third World poverty can be adequately reflected in terms of a measure by the international poverty line.

Citing Oppenheim (1993) and Townsend (1985), Wong stated that the downside in using relative and absolutist models of poverty measurement is that an absolutist definition of Third World poverty takes no account of social and cultural needs. In addition, comparative standards of poverty, as Wong points out, while relevant to fast-growing Third World economies in which subsistence poverty standards may not adequately represent rapid changes in living conditions and comparative standards in addition to the subsistence standards, could be instrumental in measuring between income inequality and economic growth.

According to Wong (1995), comparative methods of measuring poverty are relevant to some Third World nations where the governments have not "adopted an egalitarian incomes policy and the rising economic affluence might not 'trickle down' to the poor" (Wong, p. 202).

As far as the advantages of using the international poverty line in measuring Third World poverty, the average-or median-income-linked international poverty line is set at 50 percent of the average or median disposable family income in each country (Wong, 1995). According to Wong, those who fall below the income standard are considered poor. In this example, the fast-growing economy of China, under Deng Xiaoping's system of economic reform, is used as an example for exploring the use of the average-or median-income-linked international poverty line in measuring Third World poverty (Wong, 1995). In searching for underlying reasons in depicting poverty in the new millennium, Harper and Manasse (2001) initially cited several authors, in which a so-called world scale aims to measure the disposition that the world is a just place to live. Authors Harper, Wagstaff, Newton, and Harrison (1990) found that the "pro–just world" factor of the Just World Scale (JWS) correlated significantly with a so-called blame-the-poor factor of the eighteen Causes of the Third World Poverty Questionnaire (CTWPQ). Although this finding was consistent with prior research, the lack of a significant relationship between any of the JWS components in terms of the "blame exploitation" was very surprising.

Harper and Manasse (2001) argue that researchers must examine the organizational structures that, they believe, help to perpetuate poverty and to also explore how people talk about poverty and justice in daily life. For example, they cite Edelman (1977) that far from being consistent, governments and individuals instead have resources to contradictory explanations for poverty, such as a blaming discourse of the poor as well as society, and these are used at different times to perpetuate this same discourse.

The World Bank's annual World Development Report is a widely respected source of statistical information on trends in poverty and related social conditions. There and on its website, the bank reports detailed information on national accounts (e.g., GDP, income and trade data), business conditions, governmental policies, and developmental assistance in addition to the poverty data.

The UN provides similar data and a similar report: the annual and regional Human Development Report. Although much of the data is the same, the tone of the reports does reflect the ideologies of the countries in control of the organizations. The World Bank tends to see poverty as something to be addressed by economic development; the UN stresses that addressing poverty and inequality will have the side benefit of promoting economic development (see World Bank's annual World Development Report).

According to Schwabe (2004), new estimates of poverty show that the proportion of people living in poverty in South Africa has not changed significantly between 1996 and 2001. However, those households living in poverty have sunk deeper into poverty, and the gap between the rich and poor has widened. The Human Sciences Research Council (HSRC), in collaboration with Andrew Whiteford, a South African economist, has generated these estimates.

According to the Global Poverty Research Group (2010), the unemployment rate in South Africa is one of the highest in the world, rising from 36 percent to 42 percent since the year 2000. In addition, according to the GPRG, the unemployment rate for different groups reveals a tremendous disparity in the incidence of unemployment. Given the importance of employment income in total household income in South Africa, the varying incidence of unemployment across different groups has important implications for the distribution of income as well as for the incidence of poverty (here, consider Robert Kennedy's Bedford–Stuyvesant approach, which emphasized job creation as of extreme importance).

According to Blackburn (1998), despite great effort by social scientists in developing and defending various measures of poverty, no consensus has been reached on an appropriate measurement for this concept. In fact, as Blackburn points out, there is general disagreement over whether the state of the poor should be designed on the basis of some absolute needs standard or on the basis of "needs" that change as the average level of well-being increases (as cited in Atkinson, 1983; Blackburn, 1990).

Blackburn states that given this "lack of consensus, conclusions from comparisons of poverty in different countries can be quite fragile if there is insufficient exploration of the sensitivity of comparisons to the way in which poverty is operationalized." According to Blackburn, a valid scientific measurement cannot be validated regarding either an absolutist or relativistic comparison of poverty in different countries.

Author Klass (2002) begs the question: do free markets and globalization foster greater or lesser poverty and inequality in the developing world? Or according to Klass, does international development assistance to Third World nations alleviate or exacerbate the conditions of poverty? And do welfare state social policies significantly reduce poverty in developed nations? (Klass, 2002). Klass states that poverty rates generally measure the percent of the population living in households whose annual income (or, as we shall see, annual expenditures) falls below a predetermined poverty threshold.

There are two different approaches to determining the standard of living that constitutes poverty: absolute poverty thresholds define a level below which households lack basic necessary goods and services; while relative thresholds measure the percentage of the population living at a standard well below the average of their fellow citizens (Klass, 2002). According to this author, neither strategy for defining poverty is ideal. Poverty, according to Klass, is inherently a relative concept, and absolute standards are often arbitrary, while relative thresholds measure inequality more than they measure a consistent level of deprivation. For these and other reasons, according to Wood, debates about poverty often end up being debates about the measurement of poverty. Wood, citing Chossudovsky (1999) and Mangum (2003), states that liberal scholars often argue that poverty rate statistics underestimate the true dimensions of poverty, while conservatives often argue that the statistics exaggerate poverty either because the thresholds are set too low or because the measure of income and consumption do not include all the resources available to the families who are classified as poor (Rector & Hedermann, 2004).

Wood's (1998) article explores historically grounded connections between cultural and political identities and how they persist in contemporary Europe within its multicultural or "supranational" frameworks. Wood argues that nations remain at the starting point (and for many, the endpoint) for conceptions of belonging and of political legitimacy. While economic prosperity is an essential ingredient, the European project cannot be built or sustained by perceived common economic interests alone. According to Wood, in recent years, this has been realized by elites in favor of integration and has resulted in an increased concentration on the cultural dimension. Creating and psychologically implanting a formula that activates a resolute belief in a "common cultural heritage" has proven difficult, however. By comparison, historiographic influences and contemporary social referents are still overwhelmingly national in character (Wood, 1998).

According to Lancaster and Ray (2002), cross-country poverty comparisons on unit records have, rarely, involved both developing and developed countries. The present study attempts to fill this gap by comparing poverty across fourteen nations with diverse economic and demographic characteristics and at vastly different stages of economic development. Lancaster and Ray's study contains evidence on cross-country variation in the equivalence scales estimated in the presence of both household-size economies and adult/child relativities, impact of demographic adjustment of the poverty line that incorporate household size and composition changes on the poverty rates, and sensitivity of the poverty estimates and their rankings to the "equivalence elasticity." The authors' study finds that country rankings based on per capita GNP bear very little resemblance with that based on aggregate poverty rates; the latter hid substantial variation in the poverty estimates across household types.

"Growth is good for the poor" is a ubiquitous statement and one generally backed by theory, research, and history. In the long run, growth reduces poverty. Yet growth in output per se is neither a necessary nor a sufficient condition for poverty reduction in the short term. Verme uses a number of parametric and nonparametric methodologies to assess the relation between growth and poverty in Kazakhstan, a country that experienced rapid growth and poverty reduction in the short term. Combining macro-and microregional data, we find a very small trickle-down effect of output growth on household incomes and no evidence that output growth is correlated with poverty reduction (Verme, 2010). The author instead finds that poor growth in household income explains well poverty reduction.

IX

Corporate Social Responsibility

Charles Wilbur (2001) stated that to thoroughly understand the MNC, one must also understand the economic, political, and social forces that may affect the bargaining power of the modern MNC. He states that to thoroughly understand all these forces of change, one must also have an appreciation for centrality of conflict and power within that process and recognition of the importance of "nonrational" behavior. This implies that a theory of power shapes economic policies and outcomes, and this equals nonrational behavior in most cases (Wilbur, 2001).

According to Aldaceaj, Thibodeaux, and Nasif (2001), citing Kolde (1985), nation-state conflicts can be broken down into two major sources: the first one is human error, or mismanagement, by either an MNC or the host nation that it does business within; the second cause of objective conflicts occurs when MNCs and nation-states have differing goals and strategic development.

Aldaceaj et al. (2001) explained that in terms of measuring CSR, selected sources of conflicts between nation-states and MNCs may include such things as ownership structure and capital transfers—for example, according to this author, if a host country suffers a balance of payments deficit and thus restricts outbound transfer of funds: infrastructure, in terms of disagreements over the responsibility for building roads, electric power sources, water and sewer systems, and the specialization of facilities whereby the host government pressures an MNC to broaden its product line or to make more parts locally;

social behavior, whereby different cultural or social norms in home and host countries affect most seriously the communication and interactions between MNC headquarters and the affiliate managers; and taxation, whereby the host government seeks to maximize tax revenues, or they assign different values to the same transfer, requiring different systems of accounts or disregarding an MNC's tax obligations to other nations.

In reviewing the reasons just listed, Aldaceaj et al. (2001) stated that it is inevitable that a power balance exists between the MNC and the nation-state in terms of being in equilibrium. According to these authors, since power is a perceptual construct, if one of the parties in the relationship between governments and MNCs perceives itself as having more or less power and is in the hands of incompetent leaders and this leads to a situation of abuse of power, then there need to be guidelines by which parties can seek redress.

According to Aldaceaj et al. (2001), the abuse of power can be prevented if both the MNCs and host governments are socially responsible in their actions and if such voluntary action on the part of MNC leaders and managers will lead to achieving socially responsible objectives other than those dictated by market forces or imposed upon the firm by public policy. In the abuse of power scenario, this researcher would argue that these kinds of situations would be best handled by the UN for transactional companies in terms of the creation of regulatory reform as well.

The basic argument in Franklin Root's article "Environmental Risks and the Power of Multinational Corporations" (1988) is that the contextual environment consists of a multiplicity of actors linked through political, economic, technological, sociocultural, and physical interactions that can constrain the MNC's transactional interactions but does not enter into them. This may have profound implications in terms of MNCs being effective in dealing with situations of extreme poverty, such as those in Sub-Saharan Africa. According to Root, the critical distinction between the two environments is that multinational managers can influence and impact in some degree the behavior of transactional actors. On the other hand, according to this author, the contextual environment—which involves group of actors linked by political, economic, and social interactions—cannot be controlled by the MNC.

As Aldaceaj et al. (2001) pointed out, maintaining leverage with a host government involves a transactional environment where the MNC staff and actors come into contact within a new mix of risk exposure and risk-control strategies. According to these authors, the MNC's bargaining power with its host country is greatest just prior to its involvement in that country; in turn, a host country almost always wants something the MNC has, such as technology, access to world markets, management skills, capital, and other assets if appropriate. The MNC, on the other hand, usually wants access to markets, natural resources, labor, etc. from its host government (Aldaceaj et al., 2001).

As Aldaceaj et al. (2001) pointed out, once an MNC has established a venture within a host government, the host government now has the power to deprive the MNC of its venture assets through such means as price controls, taxation, local content requirements, and restriction on repatriation. In sum, according to these authors, the venture of the MNC now becomes hostage to its host government. In addition, as these authors point out, for an MNC to maintain its bargaining leverage with a host government depends upon the following:

The host government's perception that the social benefits of the MNC continue to exceed its social costs; and the host government's perception that the MNC is an indispensable source of net social benefits, a source that could not be replaced by a local entity.

What can the MNC do now to sustain the net social benefits of its venture as perceived by the government? First of all, according to Aldaceaj et al. (2001), the MNC managers must understand and not assume that they understand what the government views as socially beneficial and what it views as socially costly. In addition, according to Root (1988), sustaining the perceived net social benefits of the MNC's venture is necessary but not sufficient to maintain good relations with the host country. This is because, as Aldaceaj et al. (2001) pointed out, many host governments, particularly in developing countries, view

MNCs as foreign-owned ventures and as undesirable on purely political grounds. Thus, according to these authors, in these kinds of situations, the presence of an MNC or foreign investor can only be justified if they are making a positive social contribution that is beyond the capability of local firms.

According to Aldaceaj et al. (2001), to maintain a sense of viability in developing countries, policies that may build leverage for an MNC include the following:

Keeping local ventures dependent on inflows from parent companies that would be impossible to replace, such as technology, management skills, etc.; keeping control over local ventures' access to world markets; establishing multiple national producing (sourcing) locations for products manufactured by the joint venture; and lobbying the host government through the MNC's own contacts or the foreign business community and local business organizations.

As Viswanathan and Sridharan (2009) point out, businesses have recently begun to focus on providing market solutions for the world's poor. This article presents an alternative but complementary microlevel perspective of consumers, small-business owners or entrepreneurs, and marketplace behaviors. This perspective aims to understand and enable the subsistence marketplaces of the world to move toward becoming sustainable marketplaces—a critical goal for business and humanity. Following a brief discussion of the state-of-the-art business approach to poverty alleviation, this article presents the rationale for the sustainable marketplaces perspective, outline research, and educational and social initiatives that have emerged from taking this perspective and discusses implications for businesses that aim to take leadership in poverty alleviation.

Taking the case of the modern MNC and South Africa as its host government, the MNC needs to convince the host government that they utilize venture capital that will enhance the government's economic and social welfare. If there is a problem relating to this, the host government will have a strong tendency not to trust such an MNC. And the MNC itself, as one of the transactional actors in the equation, should demonstrate a positive social contribution. In addition, such outflows of technology and management skills should also be shared with host countries without hesitation and be willing to share the government's products (both unilaterally and bilaterally) with those of other nations in the world. Such actions as these of the modern MNC constitutes a completely open environment that is conducive to positive sources of marketing leadership in poverty alleviation. The success of both transactional actors—the MNC, and, in this case, South Africa—is heavily dependent upon an open social and economic environment and specifically implies a positive resource creation model. The authors conducted research in India to explore a complementary sociological perspective in marketplaces characterized by widespread poverty; a key finding was the existence of pervasive and highly social one-on-one relationships among interdependent consumers and sellers.

Another innovative way for small businesses to thrive in areas of global poverty, according to Uhlfelder and Lima (2005), has to do with microfinance loans offered to poor entrepreneurs. According to these authors, functions of microfinance institutions (MFIs) include collecting money from investors and offering small loans to business people in developing countries; details of money loaned by MFIs (2003) reported that the default rates on MFI loans are lower than that of U.S. lenders despite high interest rates. The benefits of microfinance loans to borrowers without access to traditional bank loans include advice to potential investors in MFIs, work of the Calvert Social Investment Foundation of Bethesda, Maryland, to promote the work of MFIs, and the social benefits of investing in MFIs. Another group of MFI entrepreneurs, in which this author has participated, is Kiva; there have been very few defaults, and most small businesses are successful in completing their business plan.

X

The Case of the European Union

This author chose to examine the EU from an organizational perspective in terms of its characteristics of innovative change, type(s) of leadership models involved in the organization, and the reason leadership hype is critical for innovative change in this organizational model. According to Dehmel (2006), the notion of lifelong learning is a concept that the EU has, in particular, promoted in terms of policy matter. As a result of being stimulated by progress toward a single European market and by the threats of worldwide terrorism as well as the opportunities afforded by globalization and new information technologies, there has been a growing interest in lifelong learning within the EU since the early 1990s (Dehmel, 2006). Thus, education is viewed as a transformational if not transcendental factor in determining positive progress concerning the EU and its market.

For example, according to Dehmel (2006), whereas the driving forces that brought lifelong learning back on an international policy agenda during the 1990s were primarily utilitarian, economic objectives, a general shift toward more integrated policies that combine social and cultural objectives with the rationale for lifelong learning can be noticed toward the middle and end of the 1990s. In turn, this would have an indirect bearing on Third World poverty.

The four basic ideas forming the basis of the EU include the free movement of goods, the free movement of persons, and the free movement of services (Usunier et al., 2005). In effect, the countries that form the EU involve a customs union in that all members have a common external tariff and customs procedure(s) vis-à-vis Third World countries (Usunier et al., 2005). With the introduction of the Maastricht Treaty in 1994, members of the EU now see themselves as coordinating and integrating economic policy as an economic union (Usunier et al., 2005). Since 1994, a part of the economic integration policy is that no individual EU country is represented in the WTO; the EU, as its own collective organization, now negotiates agreements after a discussion among member states has produced a common position (Usunier et al., 2005).

This writer's opinion regarding global poverty is that those nations that make up the EU are much more committed and engaged on a regional and international basis in combating Third World poverty. This writer believes that if there are to be significant changes in the way in which the West deals with poverty within the Third World, it will have to, at least in the beginning, involve the strong commitment of member nations of the EU. In addition, this writer argues that the United States, lacking the democratic socialistic ethic of compassionate politics and capitalistic in nature, lacks the commitment or dedication needed to be an effective force in the struggle against world poverty.

One example of the power of the EU vis-à-vis the actions of the United States: just after Pres. George W. Bush declared war on Iraq and established a unilateral foreign policy position on Iran as well as North Korea, the EU strengthened its position as the UN's most economically, politically stable and innovative force as a partner for change. According to Schori et al. (2005), while President Bush pursued a reckless course of unilateralism vis-à-vis the War in Iraq, the EU emphasized a foreign policy approach that was bilateral as well as multilateral. While the United States squandered its goodwill in terms of innovative changes on a global scale, the EU worked as an engine for positive global change, nurturing the development of democratic regimes, opening trade and investment, working to reduce poverty, and protecting the environment (Schori et al., 2005).

In terms of the EU's contributions to UN funds and programs, it comes to around 50 percent of the total budget as compared to 17 percent for the UN (Schori et al., 2005). This writer sees that in terms of fighting world poverty and terrorism, innovative changes will be needed in such areas as agricultural subsidies and technological innovations that target the problems of Third World poverty as opposed to billions and billions of dollars spent annually on military expenditures. The areas that this writer believes the EU should focus more directly upon in terms of world poverty lie in the emphasis upon technological change.

XI

Innovation in Organization and Leadership

In terms of a research project that focused upon business organizational and leadership innovations, this writer chose to examine, analyze, and evaluate Robert Kennedy's 1966 ghetto regeneration project, located in Bedford–Stuyvesant, a poor district in Brooklyn, New York. The purpose of this research was to examine the economic, political, and social implications of this project in terms of a global template at targeting Third World poverty (Sub-Saharan South Africa was chosen), for it is not due to a lack of resources that impacts global poverty; at its heart is a lack of will on the part of richer nations such as the United States as well as nations within the umbrella of the EU.

For example, in terms of characteristics of "learning organizations," which this writer believes is a good fit in dealing with the global issues of Third World poverty, its qualities, according to Cummings and Worley (2005), are mutually exclusive and fall into the following five interrelated categories:

Structure: Organization structures emphasize teamwork, lesser number of layers, strong lateral relations, and networking across organizational boundaries.

Information systems: This involves gathering and processing information in terms of facilitating rapid acquisition, sharing of rich and complex information, and helping people manage knowledge for competitive advantage.

Human resource practices: Human resources involve appraisal, rewards, and training to reinforce the acquisition and sharing of new skills and technology.

Organizational culture: Strong cultures promote openness, creativity, and experimentation among their members and encourage members to acquire, process, and share information; this also provides the underlying support for employees to nurture innovation and provides the freedom to try new things, to risk failure, and to learn from mistakes.

Leadership: The leaders of learning organizations are able to actively model that openness, risk-taking, and reflection necessary for learning; they are also to communicate a compelling vision of the learning organization and then, in turn, provide the empathy, support, and personal advocacy needed to lead others in the organization in that direction.

Jack Newfield's 1969 memoir of Robert Kennedy describes how the Bedford–Stuyvesant Restoration Corporation (BSRC), founded in 1967, became the nation's first community development corporation and, in turn, became the model for hundreds of similar groups and organizations founded throughout the United States. Newfield described the various facets of this community regeneration project, such as a low-cost home-improvement program, a mortgage loan fund, job creation and training, recruitment of businesses into the community arts programs, and health services, among others.

Hannan and Freeman (1989) argued that long-term change in the diversity of organizational forms within a population occurs through selection rather than adaptation. They believe that most organizations have structural inertia, which hinders adaptation when the environment changes. Those organizations, according to these authors, that become compatible with the environment are inevitably replaced through competition with new organizations better suited to external demands.

Bowman and Collier (2006) examined the contingency approach to resource-creation processes in terms of the power of "strategic choice" of organizations in determining their fate. They examined organizations from the perspective of resource-creation processes in terms of the competitive advantage. Citing Mintzberg (1979), Bowman and Collier argued that these two dimensions (environment and the complexity of tasks) are central in consideration of successful resource creation. These authors argue that the outcome of a strategizing activity should be a realization of a resource-creation process; a contingency theory of resource-creation processes should identify the nature of resource advantages in different contexts.

According to Scott (2003), since organizations are viewed as active and not passive agents in determining their own fate, citing Aldrich and Pfeffer (1976, p. 83), the resource-dependency model views organizations as "capable of changing as well as responding to the environment" (p. 86). Administrators manage their environments as well as their organizations, and the former activity may be even more important than the latter. Hence, it becomes a matter of power and/or politics from a pragmatic perspective. According to Scott then, the major contribution of the resource-dependency perspective has been to discern and describe the tactics ranging from buffering to diversification and merger-employed by organizations to adapt and modify their environments. It appears obvious to this writer that the larger the organization and thus the greater economies of scale, the greater the impact upon the environment(s) from a resource-dependency perspective.

It appears to this writer that many of the problems that faced the Bedford–Stuyvesant ghetto regeneration project—such as joblessness, drug abuse, and overall poverty—also face South Africa today; particularly high levels of unemployment also were the case of Bedford–Stuyvesant. Although this writer recognizes there are substantial differences between Bedford–Stuyvesant and South Africa, such as one being a district within a huge city (i.e., New York City) and the other being a nation in Sub-Saharan Africa, there are still common solutions that may be applied to both demographical and geographical areas.

Obviously, MNCs are not going to get rich in terms of foreign aid into South Africa (at least not at first), but other incentives may be available, possibly tax related (or tax incentives), as was the case in the Bedford–Stuyvesant project. However, once this was established, it would also take the combined power of the UN, the WTO, and the World Development Corporation, not to mention various interested NGOs and their allies, to develop and create the foundation or structure (whether social, economic, or political) within South Africa itself, thus eliminating poverty on a pragmatic level, perhaps a resource-dependency model would work.

In a general sense, taking all this into account, it appears to this writer that if similar organizations (corporations) were set up, as was the case in Bedford–Stuyvesant, through corporate global investment, economic development, and international foundations (along with a global Marshall Plan), the situation of dire poverty within South Africa (and other Third World economies as well) might be considerably reduced and possibly eliminated in the long run, according to the UN's Millennium Development Goals.

According to Scott (2003), resource-dependency theory assumes that one cannot understand the structure or behavior of an organization without understanding the context in which it operates. Thus, this writer argues that, as in the case of Bedford–Stuyvesant and South Africa, an organizational resource-dependency model would work best since it would work within a specific context (joblessness, housing, economic development, and poverty) as an active rather than passive agent, and also, the contingency approach to resource-creation processes looks to the power of "strategic choice" in determining its outcome.

Given Bedford–Stuyvesant's ability to adapt to the changing business environment(s), its ability to shift with the times can only serve the situation in South Africa that much better. In terms of organizational ecology and in viewing it within the perspective of an open systems paradigm relating to the struggle of global poverty, it represents a complex mixture of unseen, intangible relationships, relationships between the people and policies as well as ethics and practices of an organization (Shewchuk, 2010). It is this writer's conviction that poverty and joblessness within South Africa can only be addressed within a strategic dependency model in the short term and an ecological organizational model in the long term.

In addition, Borgatti (2010) explains how globalization is changing in terms of how businesses and organizations operate, including how they meet the needs of a changing workforce, find talent, create economic value, meet customers' needs, and fulfill social responsibilities. According to Borgatti, social-network analysis can also have a profound effect since it is grounded in the mapping and measuring of human relationships and flows among people, groups, organizations, and computer-or other information/knowledge-processing entities; in this sense, social network is the study of political and social relations among a set of actors.

Walonick (1993) argues that the environment and organizational structure is particularly important. He states that not only is the relationship important between an organization and its environment, but also, it is characterized by a two-way flow of information and energy, and in turn, organizations are open systems and depend heavily on their environment for support. For example, Walonick stated that external contingencies are economic, technological, legal, sociopoliticocultural, and environmental in nature; that is, for example, within the umbrella of external contingencies, communication is one very important factor to consider in terms of both leadership and decision making.

Borras (2004) states that the centrality of informal institutions and of meaning also relates to an interdisciplinary type of focus and perspective related to innovation. Thus, in addition to the issue of economic performance regarding MNCs, it is necessary to include political, sociological, and ecological perspectives so that the overall analysis of these organizations provides a set of holistic perspectives of system dynamics and performance in relation to the wider environment—for example, the issue of global poverty.

Elizabeth Debold (2005) describes a basic principle of transformative leadership as facing everything and avoiding nothing. She further states transformative leadership is capable of providing dramatic changes while creating huge opportunities. She describes transformational leadership as a new operating reality that is moving toward creative responsibility and embracing a "higher level of responsibility." When this writer thinks about the concept of transformational leadership, he is reminded of the mission and vision of Sen. Robert Kennedy, who transformed the ghetto of Bedford–Stuyvesant from one of hopelessness and helplessness to one in which the creativity and passion of the residents of Bedford–Stuyvesant was inspired.

According to Runte (2001), nations, cultures, languages—all are converging in the globalizing world of the early twenty-first century, giving individuals both a feeling of powerlessness and a sense of infinite possibilities; a new ethics of globalization is needed. Runte argues that the best way to create such an ethics is through education. The author proposes several ways by which students at all levels of education can achieve global awareness on a personalized basis. According to Runte, these courses would focus on global awareness and on the local solution of globally relevant problems; in turn, much of the feasibility of the simultaneous global delivery of such courses would depend on the deft use of the Internet and, in general, of the information technologies.

As a doctoral student in international relations at Argosy University, Sarasota, Florida, this writer took a course entitled Global Challenges, which focused upon the nation of South Africa, in the sub-Saharan area of Africa. For example, Padaychee (2005) pointed out that the South African government's key policy ideas centered around the supply side and especially on increasing labor-market flexibility, along with skill capacity and infrastructure investment. Padaychee believes that whatever the merits of such interventions on the supply side (and he believes that he would have difficulty in agreeing that the labor market needs to be made even more flexible), a far bolder approach is essential if higher growth, lower unemployment—which is a major cause of poverty—and reduced poverty are to be attained.

Padaychee (2005) argues that this would require a clearer and directly propoor macroeconomic stance, with some relaxation on budget deficit and inflation targets as well as some serious attention to the demand side of the economy, where evidence suggests that intervention such as the "basic income grant" should be given serious attention. Padaychee argues that the democratic government of South Africa has, over ten years, adopted an approach to the role of the state that has been an extreme reaction to what it saw (correctly) as the distortions of the apartheid state. This has been coupled with pressures coming out of the (anti-Keynesian) Washington Consensus; the government's stance appears to be based on fears about activating a demand-side role for itself. Padaychee argues that it is time to take a new look at the state in South African development, freed from these and similar paralyzing logics.

Pillay (2001) stated that the major thrust of the health-sector reform strategy of the South African government is a decentralization of services (i.e., closer to participatory grassroots democracy) from the national government to provincial and local governments. However, while much work has been done to determine new roles and responsibilities, much more work needs to be done. Pillay points out that the mechanisms to secure intergovernmental collaboration, vital to the creation of a national health system, are "embryonic and require maturation" (p. 751).

To understand why South Africa and other sub-Saharan developing countries still remain largely marginalized in terms of global trade, it is necessary to examine such combined ideologies as Westernism, unipolarism, Americanism, and globalism. Maghadelo (2005) stated that from Westernism to globalism, Africa's condition has worsened. In fact, Africa's reality contrasts sharply with the remarkable advancement in other regions in the world, such as China, India, South Korea, and Vietnam. Maghadelo argues that globalization, being unequal in its impacts and benefits, has favored the sponsors and allies of the project at the expense of Africa.

As SARPN (2010)—South African Regional Rate of Poverty—pointed out, although the proportion of people living in poverty in South Africa has diminished slightly, those households living in poverty have sunk deeper into poverty, and the gap between the rich and poor has widened. For example, SARPN pointed out that approximately 57 percent of individuals in South Africa were living below the poverty income line in 2001, a rate unchanged since 1996. According to the HSRC (2010)—Human Sciences Research Council—the group that suffers the worst unemployment rates and human capital characteristics such as education and employment service has dramatically reduced the chances of unemployment.

Looking at this information, according to the HSRC (2010), it would appear that a policy prescription that African education and skills should therefore be upgraded might not solve the problem. According to the HSRC, unless there are more jobs in the South African economy, upgrading the education of Africans will at best change the composition of employment in their favor; although there may be an increase in skilled labor within the market "clearing," the problem of unskilled labor for which there is no market clearing ends in a surplus of workers.

This writer would submit that in the case of Robert Kennedy's Bedford–Stuyvesant project, more public-housing and public-works projects could be implemented, which would require unskilled labor since new housing, apartment, and business projects would require painters, carpenter's helpers, and a whole range of building activities that would require those at the bottom of the employment process to help as assistants; at the very least, they could be educated to learn simpler building techniques, which would then free up any skilled laborers.

Maghadelo (2005) argues that to achieve development, Africa must pursue its interests independent of the forces of globalization, which have only succeeded in worsening Africa's structural dependency and marginal status in the world system. According to this author, the onus lies within the present crop of African leaders to redesign the development plan of their region and represent the continent as a worthy partner of the developed countries of Europe and America in the global network of nations.

It is only then, as Maghadelo argues, if such a design is produced, that this could lead to such schemes as the New Economic Partnership for Africa's Development. In turn, according to Maghadelo, such a scheme could transform the continent economically, politically, and socially as well as enhance development and progress in Africa. According to this author, one must start with the dismantling of structures inherited from colonialism, all of which have remained important obstacles to economic growth and development.

With regard to my doctoral research at Argosy University, doing research in organizational systems theory, Hannan and Freeman (1989) argued that long-term change in the diversity of organizational forms within a population occurs through selection rather than adaptation. They believed that most organizations have structural inertia, which hinders adaptation when the environment changes. According to Hannan and Freeman, those organizations that become incompatible with the environment are inevitably replaced through competition with new organizations that are better suited to external demands.

In examining the holistic approach to the study of organizations, Desta (2009) cites Senge (1990) in his description of systems theory in stressing the ability to view the whole world together instead of the world made up of individual fragments. These same authors are bound by invisible fabrics of interrelated actions. Desta also extensively discusses the other four disciplines that include "personal mastery," the discipline of continually clarifying and deepening our personal vision, focusing our energies, developing patience, and seeing reality objectively and, as such, which can be considered the spiritual foundation of the organization.

Gretzel's (2001) analysis of social network is based upon the assumption of the importance of relationships among interacting units. The social-network perspective encompasses theories, models, and applications that are expressed in terms of relational concepts or processes. In addition to the relational concept, Gretzel cited as important actors and their actions in terms of being viewed as interdependent rather than independent; relational ties among actors are channels for transfer or "flow" of resources. Network models focusing on individuals view the network structural environment as providing opportunities for or constraints on individual action; network models conceptualize structure (social, economic, political, etc.) as lasting patterns of relations among actors.

In terms of my doctoral coursework in solutions leadership, Carton (2008) utilized a combination of quantitative and qualitative studies to support his research. In doing so, he laid a positive foundation for any theoretical forms of models in any discussion of leadership and its implications. Carton outlined his studies according to the impact of goal dimensions on performance and satisfaction, temporal range dimension, and, among other topics, qualitative and quantitative goals. Carton cited recent theories of leadership studies that have suggested that transformational-charismatic leadership and transactional leadership, especially contingent reward leadership, should be utilized together.

Avolio (2007) discusses the theoretical approach to leadership studies in addressing how a universal form of research differs from a cultural specific form of leadership style and whether leaders are born leaders or leaders who are made. Avolio performed an in-depth study of individual leadership differences, including an integrative focus, a follower focus, and, as well, the traditional contingency models of leadership. Avolio cited Hunt and Dodge (2007) in terms of pointing toward a more integrative viewing of leadership, including genetics to cultural and generational and strategy levels, which should be considered at the outset. In addition, Avolio stated that leaders cannot be thought of as separate from the historical context in which they exist, the setting in which they function, for example, a particular city or state.

In addressing the leadership theory model, MacNeil (2006) initially stated that the leadership theory is by no means linear. In defining leadership, MacNeil stated, "Leadership is a relational process combining ability (knowledge, skills) with authority (voice, influence, and decision-making power) to positively influence and impact diverse individuals, organizations, and communities" (pp. 27–43).

MacNeil cited a variety of leadership theory models that she felt did a great job in identifying those factors related to the diversity of models with respect to adult and leadership. She elaborated on the functional framework of leadership, a feminist perspective on leadership roles, as well as a postindustrial model of leadership in discussing differences between youth development theories of leadership and adult development theories of leadership.

In terms of my doctoral coursework in ethical management, Ciulla (2005) drew her conclusions about what constitutes ethical leadership from Aristotle. For example, according to her, Aristotle defined the ultimate end of human values, for which there is no other end, as constituting happiness. Ciulla states that she found happiness more satisfactory than liberty, equality, or justice as an answer to the question "What is the end of leadership?" This solution, according to Ciulla, leads us to three general, obvious, and completely intertwined categories for the moral assessment of leadership:

The ethics of leaders themselves—the intentions of leaders and the personal ethics of leaders; the ethics of how a leader leads, the process of leadership, or the means that a leader uses to lead (the ethics of the relationship between leaders and all those affected by their actions); and the ethics of what a leader does—that is, the ends of leadership.

These three parts encompass virtue theory and deontological and teleological approaches to ethics (Ciulla, 2005). In addition, according to Ciulla, they also run parallel to some of the major areas of social-science research on leadership.

XII

Investment in Human and Social Capital

This writer believes that although investment in physical capacity is a better bet in terms of physical capacity not breaking down like human capital, various studies show that the more business investment in both human and social capital, the greater will be the return on earnings. In addition, the greatest utility gotten from investments in human and social capital appears to be in the realm of both postsecondary schools as well as higher education (Nitzan & Paroush, 1980). According to Nitzan and Paroush, the greater one's investment in human capital, the smaller the probability of error, and in fact, this model of investment in human capital plays the same role as a hedge against risk in the form of "self-protection"; in addition, this implies that it is actually in the public interest to invest in members of society.

If one is to argue that business-investment decisions in either social or human capital are something more beneficial than not, then one cannot ignore the interdisciplinary ramifications of the impact of economics on contemporary sociology. To begin with, while traditional sociological theory implies that any theory can be reduced to individual human action (in turn cannot be fodder for sociological study), human capital theory (Becker, 1964) has probably influenced sociology more than any other economic theory (Baron & Hannan, 1994).

According to Baron and Hannon (1994), the core contribution of human capital theory was to couch education, health, and other behaviors in investment terms. These investment terms included rates of return (and thus the life cycle), opportunity costs, funding of investments (capital constraints), and the ability of the investor to realize returns from the investment. For example, according to Baron and Hannan (1994), sociologists utilized the language of markets without always specifying a structure of investment or depreciation. In turn, according to these authors, the influence of schooling on earnings became labeled consequences of education. Thus, sociologists examining labor markets felt that they must control for "human capital variables," and the effects of education on careers came to be considered as an instance of human capital economics (Baron & Hannon, 1994). However, in the end, sociologists became disenchanted with the utilization of economic terms in discussing sociological theory and practice.

After much debate and consideration, Baron and Hannan (1994) point out that sociologists decided they were much more comfortable in drawing conclusions about the trend in the impact of economics on sociology. Baron and Hannan give several examples; in terms of sociologists disavowing assumptions of profit maximization and hyperrationality, many now assume that social behavior is strategic and goal directed. From this vantage point, recent sociological work has tried to not only situate but also examine economic actions and relations in their broader social context (Baron & Hannan, 1994).

And here is where sociology may provide much greater insight into investments of a social or human nature in terms of capital. By specifying how historical, cultural, political, social, and psychological forces impact business leaders in terms of making certain business investments more viable than others and also by articulating the sources of resistance to change in social systems, sociologists can make the study of economics more predictable (Baron & Hannon, 1994).

In making decisions of an ethical nature (e.g., investments directed toward economic development on a global level) with respect to human or social capital, all too often, these same decisions are made according to whether or not success is achieved through an emphasis upon the pragmatic ends or results. However, according to Minkler (1999), this kind of emphasis upon utility maximization does not take into account that some acts arise from a sense of duty and commitment. For example, according to Minkler, since some actions result not from utility maximization or consequentialist ends but instead from a commitment to moral interests or motivations, a better framework should be developed that includes models devoted to people who act out of altruistic motivations versus the standard economic model that basically implies that all individuals act in an opportunistic manner to benefit individual self-interest.

Minkler (1999) goes on to describe Immanuel Kant's ethical system, which basically argues that the means or philosophy of instrumentality is far more important than achieving pragmatic ends since it is impossible to state with certainty that one's actions will result in the desired ends. Thus, according to Minkler (1999), Kant's ethical framework implies that the highest good is to follow one's moral duties, and thus, motivations do not play a role for Kant.

However, to counter Kant's ethical framework, Minkler (1999) cites W. D. Ross; promoting Kant's emphasis upon moral duty, in turn, implies that it is not quite as simple as all that. Ross goes on to point out that various duties in and of themselves may at times conflict so that what you really need is an ethical ranking of duties and motives. Finally, according to Minkler (1999), much exploration needs to be done in this area. He states that while commitment, for example, is considered both virtuous and clear-cut, in the real world, life is seldom so simple.

For example, according to Hinkler, economists often suggest that promise keeping in transactions can only be assured if a reputational asset is at stake; he also states even if reputational assets are related to promise keeping, that does not mean the link is causal. Perhaps reputational assets are the result, while commitment is the cause, at least in some cases. If this is correct, according to Hinkler, we may be incorrectly identifying the true sources for a well-functioning economy. In that case, we can only profit from a further study of human capital commitment's characterization but also, in turn, the values and institutions that nurture and sustain it.

This writer has tried to show that while some authors relegate human capital to an emphasis upon physical capital in terms of possible utility value, this writer also feels that investments in human and social capital not only make good ethical sense but also make good business and economic sense. This argument furthers the notion that investments in economic development in Third World countries are a very positive rather than negative approach to decision making.

The study of economic sociology has also become an increasingly important method of predicting human activity, whether in social groups or within an economic perspective. In addition, investment(s) in human capital, according to this research, seems to say that investment in postsecondary and higher education produces the greatest result economically; in addition, this writer argues that investments in human capital have a compensatory social value as well as greater value in business investment (stock) returns.

XIII

An International Code of Ethics

One of the main questions one must examine on a national and/or international and global level is whether it is even possible or, for that matter, feasible for any MNC to adhere to a given set of ethical guidelines both in terms of its corporate employees and also one that can rule the actions (a code, if you will) of a corporation's marketing department. This writer believes that it is not only possible to do so but also incumbent upon a multinational corporate culture to follow a series of ethical guidelines to carry us forward through the twenty-first century.

Before drawing up a code of specific ethical guidelines for a corporate marketing department, I also feel it is important to provide a philosophical basis for such a code so that all marketing employees as well as employees of other departments will better understand the reasons behind doing so. For example, Benhabib's study (as cited by Hutchinson, 2004) argues against strong pluralist responses to the claims of culture in which different rights are accorded or assigned on the basis of cultural membership and instead argues for a more deliberative democratic solution to the accommodation of differences, both within liberal democratic states and also broadly across the global arena. This writer argues that this type of solution would be best accorded through democratic socialism or participatory democracy.

Benhabib's study (as cited by Hutchinson, 2004), with regard to a kind of international ethical presence, utilizes the phrase "weak transcendentalism" in terms of the difficulty of placing any necessary constraints on the form of justificatory strategies as having a rational basis and instead argues for a more moderate form of a "historically enlightened universalism," in turn utilizing such phrases as "universal respect" and "egalitarian reciprocity," in which all global participants and/or multinational organizations are accorded equal rights of participation and all are committed to understanding from the other's perspective. Only when wealthy businessmen and speculators feel that they have gained their share of the market economy is any thought toward social gain considered.

The next area I would like to discuss on a more philosophical level is the importance of education in terms of maintaining a healthy international ethical presence on a global level vis-à-vis MNC. We have already discussed in an earlier section how investment(s) in human and social capital, compared to physical capacity, rewards a much greater rate of return. In terms of this, corporate emphasis upon postsecondary and higher education not only targets virtuous actions but also quite often supports the view of individual moral duty, according to Immanuel Kant.

To give you a bit more of a philosophical perspective on all this, Runte (2001) cites Cameron and Stein, in describing the "weakening of national identities," argue that a "strengthened global identity, drawing on shared cultures and values and more vibrant local political identities, could provide valuable focal points for political action and institution building." Runte (2001) cites Paul Kennedy, who states the single point on which all proponents and critics of globalization agree is on the need for a new type of ethical code within the international sphere of globalization. Runte (2001) cites Kennedy in stating, "Because we are members of world citizenry, we need to equip ourselves with a system of ethics, a sense of fairness, and a sense of proportion as we consider ways in which, collectively or individually, we can be better prepared for the twenty-first century." The internal ethical code related to a corporate's marketing program includes such issues as the following:

Respect for the concerns of all individuals, whether it has to do with such things as occupational health and safety, must be maintained.

The issue of respect for everyone's human rights must be maintained at all times, including the rights of workers in offshore parts of the supply chain.

Unfair or dishonest business and accounting practices will not be tolerated and could be punishable by loss of job or, in more serious cases, taken up with a corporate internal review board.

Environmental rules of protection must always be respected.

Marketing department staff must be encouraged to have involvement within the corporate culture as well.

Consumer protection is perhaps one of the most important rules that must, at all times, be abided by.

Finally, all employees, whether at the top or at middle and lower levels of the marketing department, must follow a specific code of ethics and values (Dunham, 2002, p. 103).

In terms of an international code of ethics for MNCs, this writer submits that they should inevitably have to follow a code of ethical law or behavior that will guide their actions and decisions in dealing with a multicultural global society. That a group of ethical guidelines for MNCs be adopted on an international scale, these same guidelines should be enforced by a higher law, perhaps as an adjunct or an independent apparatus of the UN or possibly the World Bank or IMF or any combination of all three.

For example, one may cite a speech given by President Clinton regarding the mission and/or vision of the UN, that the ideals of the UN Charter—including peace, tolerance, and prosperity—are even more needed than they were ever in the past as all human beings and players throughout the global spheres are faced with new threats such as threats from terrorists of rogue nations, threats from ethnic, religious, racial, and tribal hatreds, threats from international criminals and drug traffickers, and the fact that dangerous rogue nations might gain access to weapons of mass destruction (Clinton, *Essential Speeches*, 2009).

In addressing the need for responsible transformative leadership, citing Debold (2005), it is perhaps one of the most important concepts in the struggle against global poverty; in addition, there are a variety of philosophies of a political and social nature that draw connections to one another. First of all, since there are so many factors involved in Third World poverty, it is perhaps necessary to draw a set of parameters regarding research as to what the most essential or important priorities are in dealing with this issue in the short term—or, essentially, right away—and other priorities that can possibly wait as longer goals or objectives in dealing with Third World poverty.

In addition to the political, social, and economic problems of the concept of global poverty, there is also a moral duty or issue that must be addressed in terms of a spiritual nature or within the framework of moral duties that constitute the moral-spiritual spectrum of human existence. In terms of priorities, from the spiritual perspective of Maitreya, the essential needs of all individuals or human beings should include affordable housing for all, health care, and the right to education as universal rights as well as the restoration of the environment and establishment of world peace.

This writer, in addressing the views of Maitreya, argues that all these priorities are, in some way, connected. For example, among the 4.4 billion people who live in developing nations, nearly three in five live without basic sanitation; nearly one in three are without safe drinking water (*Share International*, 2009). In addition, according to *Share International*, one quarter lack adequate housing, one in five live beyond the reach of modern health services, one in five children are undernourished, and an equal percentage do not get beyond grade five in school; even in the United States, the world's wealthiest society, some twelve million families are at risk of hunger, and at least seven hundred thousand people are homeless on any given night. According to Maitreya, this growing divide between the wealthy and the poor threaten us all as the resulting crime, social unrest, civil war, illegal immigration, and environmental degradation do not respect national or local boundaries (*Share International*, 2009).

XIV

Social Business

The newest efforts to combat global and Third World poverty have to do with the notion of social business. According to Muhammad Yunus (2007), a social business is not a profit-maximizing business (PMB); in terms of its organizational structure, the difference between a social business and a PMB is that it differs in objectives. As in the case of a PMB, which strives for greater profits, "a social business is defined by its ability to create social benefits for the lives it touches" (p. 22).

According to the author, unlike NPOs and foundations that rely upon charitable contributions or donations, a social business strives for "full cost recovery or more, even as it concentrates on creating products or services that provide a social benefit. It pursues this goal by charging a price or fee for the products or services it creates" (Yunus, 2007, p. 22).

In addition, a social business cannot exist if it does not recoup its costs fully; however, once a social project is self-sustaining, it then transcends a charitable enterprise into the world of business. Hence, the project is self-sustaining and can now legitimately be called a social business.

According to Yunus (2007), there are two kinds of social businesses. The first type focuses on providing a social benefit, such as poverty reduction, social justice, economic development, increased health care, and sustainability, providing the investors with psychological and spiritual satisfactions rather than financial reward.

The second type of social benefit seeks financial rewards for the poor and disadvantaged and, in turn, goes to the poor and disadvantaged, thus helping the disadvantaged to transcend their poverty. The financial rewards thus go to ownership, and the goods or services created provide an economic and/or social benefit.

Several years ago, this writer invested into a social business enterprise entitled Kiva. Kiva was of the second type of social benefit. As far as investment(s), one could lend as little as $25, which I did, to maximize loans, and these loans went for a variety of reasons, whether it be loans for entrepreneurs of small businesses, and again, these loans covered an entire range of smaller businesses.

My experience with Kiva is that out of a loan of twenty-five to thirty different kinds of smaller businesses, this writer can safely say that perhaps only two to three at the most failed to repay their loans. In addition, this writer should stress that all these Kiva loans went to individuals who were poor and/or disadvantaged. Thus, with the successes of the Kiva program, this writer received an emotional and/or spiritual boost or feeling; it was a very rewarding experience.

Would Maitreya, for example, support Yunus's vision of a self-sustaining social business? He obviously would support the notion of trying to create businesses that are geared toward ending poverty as we know it. The implications of this, according to Stephen Smith, professor at Washington University, relate to ending gender discrimination, social exclusion, lack of access to health care and education, eliminating environmental degradation, and, as well, ending political and/or social inequality.

For all these reasons, Yunus's book would obviously find great support from Maitreya, although the notion of a social-business stock market, where individual investors invest in the most successful social businesses, would perhaps baffle him. To try and end political and social inequalities across the globe, why would one want to create a separate social stock market that would rate social businesses in terms of being economically successful from a business or financial set of perspectives? You are essentially exchanging one type of stock market for another kind of stock market, both of which stress a financial set of perspectives. It doesn't make sense from an altruistic or aesthetic perspective. However, the social stock market operates like a traditional stock market where investors can choose among a variety of businesses (e.g., both social and regular profit-making businesses), and obviously, the potential investor will invest in the type of business that will satisfy their short-or long-term goals, whether it be social or profit-making businesses.

XV

Capitalist versus Democratic Socialist Economy

While capitalistic societies such as the United States, China, South America, and the Far East have been flourishing in the twenty-first century, there has also been great disillusionment on a global scale with the global distribution of resources. For example, as Yunus points out, 94 percent of world income go to 40 percent of the people; on the other hand, 60 percent of the rest of the people must live on 6 percent of the income. "Half of the world lives on two dollars a day or less, while almost a billion people live on less than one dollar a day" (Yunus, p. 3). However, while government, on the one hand, can do much to address social problems, on the other hand, they can be inefficient, slow, bureaucratic, prone to corruption, and self-perpetuating. (p. 8).

Still, in comparing the free-market system and its paradigm of profitability with democratic socialism and its emphasis upon social gain, a system of democratic socialism, as a form of government, works best in helping the poor and dispossessed. This writer believes that capitalism, by its very nature, is self-destructive in the sense that it only caters to the very rich, thus, in turn, creating huge pockets of inequality, while democratic socialism, by its very nature, implies, among other things, total equality of all individuals, a governmental right to intervene in society, and, if necessary, addresses social injustice. In addition, it can also address such issues in the economy as taxation, regulation, redistribution, and public ownership. This has obvious implications for marketing across cultures throughout the world, given the current problems associated with free-market capitalism.

With the onset of the recession in 2008, in many ways, the financial institutions of the United States such as Bank of America and Citigroup had already been de facto nationalized by the infusion of taxpayer equity "whose value swamps that of these firms' market equity" (dsausa.org, 2009, pp. 1–2). If one is truly examining the state of our economy in the United States, after the onset of the 2008–2009 recession, it is very hard to put on a positive face vis-à-vis our free-market capitalistic system of government. In fact, Obama's new plan actually proposed that the federal government create a private market for those toxic assets, where none now exists, by spending hundreds of billions of taxpayer dollars to write "insurance" guaranteeing a floor price to private investors who buy them (dsausa.org, 2009). Since the 2008 recession, the problems that led to the recession could occur again. These problems within the financial systems of our largest cities are basically the result of obsession and greed; it is a direct result of an economic system of capitalism that went completely haywire. Maitreya believes that the best of capitalism and the best of socialism should be combined to find the appropriate type of economic and social system: democratic socialism.

I quote one source in attempting to describe why so many of these financial institutions and other assets carried on balance sheets have left banks and shadow financial instruments such as hedge funds and private mortgage lenders are owed their depositors more than they are worth (dsausa.org, 2009). In addition, in terms of the inadequacy of our capitalistic system to work in a twenty-first-century global system, the disastrous experience of financial deregulation demonstrates that with absent public regulatory restraint, finance capital will engage in irresponsible acts of speculative swindling during financial booms and resort to excessively conservative lending practices during times of financial busts (2009).

However, the final truth of this entire mess of "neoliberal capitalism," which lies behind this economic crisis, involves product workers across the globe who are no longer paid enough to purchase the same goods and services they produce; this resulted in a Western working class who borrowed excessively against inflated home values, and in addition, the exploited working classes of China and Southeast Asia subsidized Western living standards. In turn, their governments managed the market so as to run massive trade surpluses and invested them not in domestic needs within the United States but in U.S. Treasury bonds and private equity (2009).

This writer believes that we are actually seeing the twilight of our capitalistic economic system, borne out of greed, at the expense of the working classes and that the only alternative in terms of addressing global poverty is a democratic socialist economy, which markets social gain. According to the Democratic Socialists of America, the restoration of a stable global economic system will necessitate raising the floor on global living standards and working conditions that insure that investment and trade benefit the working class of the world:

> The era of deregulatory free-market mania is crashing down on us. Only by reviving the capacity of democratic governments to regulate the economy so that it serves the peoples' needs rather than the speculative desires of corporate elites will we ever recover from the current global economic nightmare. (2009)

My argument is, how can we effectively have a free-market capitalistic system in marketing across differing cultures on a global scale when we (the United States) cannot even manage to sustain itself economically and, in fact, helped create this debacle, the recession of 2008, which is still affecting nations across the globe? One article this writer submitted was "Capitalism is hamstrung by greed." In answering a question regarding an "opinion" piece of December 22, Paul Whiteley of the Christian Science Monitor stated, "Democracy in America is broken and in need of repair. Individual and corporate greed are the chief causes of the poor state of our economy" (Whiteley, 2008, p. 8).

XVI

Political Ethics and the International Order

According to Hans Ulrich (2007), any political theory or political ethics must approach the global world as a political unity to the extent that global effects of any set of processes and/or actions are taken into account (Ulrich, 2007, pp. 5–12). Given the deep differences between traditions and narratives of political thinking and the implications that they might have upon a system of marketing, whether through market-driven capitalism or through democratic socialism (social gain), presently, no consensus exists for a particular or specific political philosophy (Ulrich, 2007). However, it must be stressed that this form of democratic socialism has nothing to do with either Marxist notions of the "dictatorship of the proletariat" or the state-sponsored socialism that was perverted in the name of Stalinist dictatorial aims.

However, as Ulrich points out, as the theme of political ethics and international order sets out a specific direction, there must be a search for an explicitly ethical view of politics on a global level. He feels that ongoing debate about ethics in "international order" or even the building of an "international order" is demanded by not only the urgent issues and facets of transnational, interconnections, which presently unsettle given democratic structures, but also the social justice philosophy, as evidenced by many Christians as well as other religious groups today who are privileged to hope for and, in turn, are fulfilled by its message (Ulrich, 2007).

Ulrich (2007) goes on to state that any search for a world order is still based upon a political engagement of people (possibly participatory democracy on an ideological level) who have not resigned from a citizenship of doing justice and making peace and whose political ethics is based upon an ethos that has been witnessed by citizens who are experienced in the Christian notion of social justice and are living together in peace and justice (Ulrich, 2007).

This author argues while capitalist culture is driven by the profit motive and is created and controlled by the corporate elite, socialist culture is created by the people for the benefit and enjoyment of the people (Beghdoyan, 2006, pp. 232–236). As we have just witnessed within the United States, capitalist rules of greed and profit maximization have led to global economic poverty and cultural devastation (Beghdoyan, 2006).

But how do we realistically go from being the world's greatest capitalistic society into a society that implies all the values of democratic socialism without having been forced into a new political and economic order as a result of a terrifying recession, which has now deeply troubled most Americans? However, as a result of nations, languages, and cultures all converging within a system of twenty-first-century globalization, giving individuals a feeling of powerlessness, it has also given individuals a sense of infinite possibilities (Runte, 2001, pp. 39–46).

R. E. Zelnik (2003), who cites G. Eley, points out that true democracy involves the active extension of citizenship rights, especially the franchise of voting rights, to all segments of the population and the enrichment of modes of political participation through the extension of fundamental rights such as free speech, freedom of the press, and the right to organize. Although we in the United States have a written constitution that perfectly spells out these same rights, we also know, if we are to be true to our best selves, that it exists only in word and not in reality.

It is my contention that to best realize these fundamental rights (vis-à-vis a system of true democracy, ethos), it might best be solved, at least in the beginning, through "participatory democracy" so that people feel that they have a say in the kind of government that sustains them—that is, a decentralized ideology of local democracy, or as Thomas Jefferson wrote, "that government that governs least governs best" (Newfield, 1988, pp. 36–37). From a perspective of decentralized participatory democracy, a democratic socialist government, according to Lewis Mumford, affords the people the ability to face one another and as well have programs that afford all human beings an adequate supply of "food, housing for all, health care, and education as universal rights," "restoration of the environment," and the "establishment of peace" (Maitreya, 2016).

According to Crème, the best form of government is that closest to the people at the local level, all political affairs decided by local people who know best what their needs are. In other words, according to Crème, the need for people for self-advancement, for freedom, and for self-determination should be conducted on the local level (Crème, p. 87). In terms of people influencing national priorities, according to Crème, this can only be done by people participating on the local level (p. 87). Decentralization, according to Crème, is the most humane form of government for people at the local level as those individuals know what priorities best serve them at this level rather than a huge federal bureaucracy.

Although the importance of a democratic socialist political economy might work best in terms of focusing upon world poverty (particularly Third World), other authors believe that the MNC will be the primary engine for eliminating world poverty in the future. Even though within the past ten years, MNOs as a whole have made attempts to enhance CSR particularly in Africa and South America, among other regions, obviously, there is still a long way to go. However, one of the main propellers of this greater focus upon CSR by MNCs as a whole, at the present time, is more of a slow evolution in the way MNCs, NGOs, and globalization interact with one another. At any rate, MNCs have come to a much greater recognition that they must gain a greater sense of legitimacy to underdeveloped nations throughout the world if they are to maintain their way in the world of globalization as well as being observed by a growing group of NGOs.

XVII

Conclusion

In discussing Third World and global poverty, I would never have taken up the cross with regard to this until I became educated and, in turn, inspired by Maitreya. Three or four years ago, after I had given up hope in terms of my Catholicism, which, in the end, I could not accept, my counselor lent me a book to read about Maitreya. His global awareness was just the kind of philosophy that appealed to me. Benjamin Crème (overshadowed by Maitreya) discussed both the economic and political implications that Maitreya supports. However, as stated earlier in this book, the tenets of Catholicism concerning the service of social justice ideals makes a strong connection with the social and economic justice as advocated by Maitreya.

On a political level, according to Maitreya, the greater the degree of decentralization of government, the better; local government where individuals can play a vital role in determining their lives is the best kind of government. This is a kind of face-to-face grassroots democracy where people participate on a local level—in other words, what is known as participatory democracy. Thus, on an economic level, people who participate in local grassroots democracy can determine what local resources are needed to provide social welfare and local health care how much funding is needed for local police authority and, in general, the needs of local community funding.

Several years back, I wrote a book entitled *Politics in Compassion*. In that book, I addressed the problems endemic in the modern world, including racism and white privilege, the care and treatment of the elderly, the issue of welfare reform, and, as well, the problems of adolescence and adolescent treatment. I also believe that most if not all these issues have a bearing on the notion of ending poverty as we know it. In that book, I addressed the compassion of Jesus Christ, which, from a political and social perspective, best addresses what I term "politics in compassion" or that type of political system that affords all individuals to have the ability for self-advancement and self-determination.

However, for the poorest of the masses on a global level to achieve these same ideals, Maitreya believes that the resources of the entire earth need to be addressed on a sharing basis; presently, millions of people starve each day on a global level. Until this major global problem is addressed, Maitreya takes a rather dim or dark view of what lies ahead for humanity as a whole. While Maitreya does what he can in terms of reaching out to the poorest of the global masses, he and his masters cannot infringe upon the free will of human beings, so this problem needs to be addressed and ultimately solved by human beings.

To begin with, according to Lodge and Wilson (2006), the legitimacy of the MNC is in question in terms of its relationship with communities throughout the Third World of global poverty. According to these authors, since the corporations are the major drivers of globalization, it is now expected of them to address the problems of poverty within the communities and to find pragmatic ways of alleviating that poverty. In terms of a problem of legitimacy, since the eradication of poverty often calls for abrupt change in the context of the poor country, it threatens to overturn the status quo, and this is a radical notion; the paradox created by this situation is that the corporation, to revive its legitimacy, "is expected to do what in many ways is illegitimate" (Lodge & Wilson, p. 163).

According to Lodge and Wilson (2006), the remedy lies in not only such organizations as the UN, NGOs, the World Bank, and similar organizations but also "to serve community needs, that is, reduce poverty without threatening its survival as a profit-making institution" (p. 163). These same authors believe that is what the World

Development Corporation could succeed at. These authors don't deny that its creation might be "precarious" and arouse suspicions on all sides, but if it could create a pragmatic link between the corporation and the other poverty reduction organizations as well as within the poor country itself, this might be an experiment that could stand the test of time (Lodge & Wilson, p. 163).

References

Abraham, D. (1994). Persistent acts and compelling norms: Liberal capitalism, democratic socialism and the law. *Law & Society Review, 28*(4), pp. 939–946.

Administration of William J. Clinton (1999). United States–European Union summit statement on the World Trade Organization, pp. 2633–34.

Aldaceaj, J., Thibodeaux, M. S., & Nasif, E. G. (2001). A power model of multinational corporation — Nation-state relationships. *SAM Advanced Management Journal,* 11.

Avolio, B. J. (2007). Promoting more integrative strategies for leadership theory-building. *American Psychologist, 62*(1), pp. 25–33.

Blackburn, M. L. (1998). The sensitivity of international poverty comparisons. *Review of Income & Wealth, 44*(4), pp. 449-472. Retrieved from EBSCO database.

Borgatti, S. (2010). Social network analysis: Introduction and resources. Retrieved on June 7, 2010, from http://ir.ed.uiuc.

Borras, S. (2004). Analytical framework: System of innovation theory and the European Union. *Science & Public Policy, 31*(6), pp. 425–433.

Bowman, C., & Collier, N. (2006). A contingency approach to resource-creation processes. *International Journal of Management, 8*(4), pp. 119–211. Retrieved from EBSCO database.

Bush, G. W. (2006). Message to the senate transmitting the United States–European Union agreement on mutual legal assistance, pp. 1677–78.

Carton, A. M. (2008). Enhancing leadership theories with goal structure. *Duke University Fuqua School of Business*. Durham, NC: Duke University, pp. 1–6.

Ciulla, J. B. (2005). The state of leadership ethics and the work that lies before us. *Business Ethics: A European Review*. Oxford, UK: Blackwell Publishing Ltd.

Clinton, B. (2006). Remarks by the president in address to the fifty-first General Assembly of the United Nations. *Essential Speeches*. Retrieved on January 29, 2009, from http://web.ebscohost.com/ehost/delivery?(This is correct footnote according to changes). It came from web.ebscohost.

Clinton, W. J. (1998). United States–European union statement on cooperation in the global economy, *34*(51), p. 2503.

Cooper, J. (1998). A multidimensional approach to the adoption of innovation. *Management Decision, 36*(8), p. 493. Retrieved October 14, 2009, from ABI/INFORM Global.

Craig, D., & Porter, D. (2005). The third way and the Third World: Poverty reduction and social inclusion strategies in the rise of "inclusive" liberalism. *Review of International Political Economy, 12*(2), pp. 226–263.

Crème, B. (2008). About Maitreya Project. Retrieved January 29, 2009, from (Correct footnote) ttp://www.maitreyaproject.org/en/project/about.html

Crème, B (1997). Maitreya's Mission. (3rd ed.). Los Angeles, CA: Share International Foundation.

Cummings, T. G., & Worley, C. G. (2005). *Organization development and change*. (9th ed.). Mason, OHH: South-Western Cengage Learning.

Dalton, M. (2009). What's constraining your innovation? *Research Technology Management, 52*(5), pp. 52–64. Retrieved October 14, 2009, from EBSCOhost database.

Davilla, T., Epstein, M. J., & Shelton, R. (2006). *Making work: How to manage it, measure it, and profit from it.* (1st ed.). Upper Saddle River, NJ: Pearson Education Inc.

Dehmel, A. (2006). Making a European area of lifelong learning a reality? Some critical reflections on the European Union's lifelong learning policies. *Comparative Education, 42*(1), pp. 49–62.

Democratic Socialists of America. (2009). What is democratic socialism? Retrieved on April 24, 2009, from http://faculty.maxwell.syr.edu/merupert/Research/far-right/dem_soc.htm.

Desta, Y. (2009). Does the EPLF (Eritrean People's Liberation Front) qualify to be a learning organization? A modern systems theory perspective. *Journal of Organizational Transformation and Social Change, 6*(1). 5-28. Retrieved from EBSCO database.

Dolgoff, R. (2009). What does social welfare produce? *International Social Work, 42*(3), pp. 95–307.

Dorrien, G. (2000). Michael Harrington: Socialist to the end. Retrieved on June 28, 2009, from http://www.religion-online.org/showarticle.asp?title=1969.

Dunham, A. (2002). Corporate ethics and restoring public confidence. *Vital Speeches of the Day*, pp. 101–105.

Font, C. (2008). The true soul of the United Nations. *Share International Archives*. Retrieved September 5, 2008, from http://www.share-international.org/ARCHIVES.

Francis, J. (2008). An idea that can bring us together. Interview with Howard Zinn. *Share International Archives*. Retrieved on September 5, 2008, from http://www.share-International.org./ARCHIVES/cooperation/co_howard-Zinn-interview.htm.

GPRD. (2010). Unemployment, race and poverty in South Africa. *Global Poverty Research Group*. Retrieved on June 14, 2010, from http://www.grpd.org/themes.

Gilpin, R. (2001). *Global political economy*. (1st ed.). Princeton, NJ: Princeton University Press.

Gretzel, U. (2001). Social network analysis: Introduction and resources. Retrieved on June 7, 2010, from http://Irs.ed.uiuc.edu/tse-portal/analysis/socialnetwork-analysis.

Hannon, M. T., & Freeman, J. (1989). Organization and social structure in organizational ecology. *Harvard University Press*, pp. 3–27. Retrieved on June 3, 2010, from http://faculty.babson.edu.

Harper, D. J., & Manasse, P. R. (2001). The just world and the third world: British explanations for poverty abroad. *The Journal of Social Psychology, 132*(6), pp. 783–785.

Hesselbein, F., Goldsmith, M., & Somerville, I. (2002). Eds. *Leading for innovation and organizing for results.* (1st ed.). San Francisco, CA: Jossey-Bass.

Hoffberg, M. (2006). Overturning the Jeffrey Sachs prescription: Impediments and consequences to the United Nation's poverty reduction strategy. (Doctoral dissertation). Argosy University online. EBSCO database.

Hutchings, K. (2004). From morality to politics and back again: Feminist international ethics and the civil-society argument. *Alternatives, 29,* pp. 239–245.

Joy, C. (2009). Recurring questions on Third World development. Retrieved October 19, 2009, from http://www.share-international.org.

Kekic, L. (2008). Twenty years of capitalism: Was it worth it? *The Economist,* pp. 94–95.

Kenworthy, L. (1999). Do social welfare policies reduce poverty? A cross-national assessment. *Social Forces, 77*(3), pp. 1119–1130.

Klass, G. (2002). Presenting data: Tabular and graphic display of social indicators. Retrieved on March 21, 2010, from http://lilt.ilstu.edu/.

Klass, G. (2002). Measuring poverty and inequality. *Illinois State University.* Retrieved on March 21, 2010, from http://lilt.ilstu.edu/ gmklass/ pos138/ datadisplay/ sections/ poverty/ poverty.html.

Lan, Z., & Anders, K. K. (2000). A paradigmatic view of contemporary administration research: An empirical test. *Administration & Society, 32*(2), pp. 138–165.

Leach, M. (2009). The needs of the poor come first — Interview with Devaki Jain. *Share International.* Retrieved on January 1, 2010, from http://www.share-international.org/ARCHIVES/hunger poverty/hp_mi-needs.

Lodge, G., & Wilson, C. (2006). *A corporate solution to global poverty.* (1st ed.). Princeton, NJ: Princeton University Press.

Lodge, G. C. (2002). Using big business to fight poverty. Retrieved January 10, 2008, from http://hbswk.hbs.edu/item/3050.html.

Lyons, G. M. (1977; 1986). Reforming the United Nations. *ISSJ, XXIX*(1).

MacNeil, A. A. (2008). *Bridging generations: Applying "adult" leadership theories to youth leadership development.* Los Angeles, CA: University of California.

Maghadelo, J. O. (2005). Westernism, Americanism, unipolarism, globalism and Africa's marginality. *Journal of Third World Studies, 22*(2), pp. 89–101. Retrieved from EBSCOhost.

Marquand, R. (2009). Europe listens cautiously to Obama agenda. *Christian Science Monitor, 101*(51), pp. 1–11.

MacDonald, S. B. (2005). Rethinking Europe's culture of entitlement. *Society*, pp. 7–8.

McSwite, O. C. (1997). Postmodernism and public administration's identity crisis. *Public Administration Review, 57*(2). Retrieved from Business Source Review.

Minkler, L. (1999). The problem with utility: Toward a non-consequentialist/utility theory synthesis. *Review of Social Economy, 107*, pp. 4–21.

Mudambi, R., Mudambi, S., & Navarra, P. (2007). Global innovation in MNCs: The effects of subsidiary self-determination and teamwork. *Product Development & Management Association, 24*, pp. 442–455.

Muller, D., & Stoger, M. (2009). Global Marshall Plan — A planetary contract. Retrieved October 19, 2009, from http://www.share-international.org.

Newfield, J. (1969). *Robert Kennedy: A memoir.* (1st ed.). New York, NY: Penguin Books.

Nitzan, S., & Paroush, J. (1980). Investment in human capital and social self-protection under uncertainty. *International Economic Review, 21*, pp. 547–557.

PR Newswire (2009). IFMR capital and equitas conclude first-ever rated securitization of microloans in India. Retrieved on March 31, 2010, from http://proquest.umi.com/pqdweb?.

Padaychee, V. (2005). The South African economy, 1994–2004. *Social Research, 72*(3), pp. 549–574. Retrieved from EBSCOhost.

Pillay, Y. (2001). The impact of South Africa's new constitution on the organization of health services in the post-apartheid era. *Journal of Health Politics, Policy and Law, 26*(4), pp. 747–766. Retrieved from EBSCOhost.

Robison, L. J., Schmid, A. A., & Stiles, M. E. (2002). Is social capital really capital? *Review of Social Economy, 110*, pp. 1–21.

Rohr, R. (2013). *Everything belongs: The gift of contemplative prayer.* (3rd ed.). New York: Crossroad Books Publishing.

Root, F. R. (1988). Environmental risks and the bargaining power of multinational corporations. *The International Trade Journal, III*(2), pp. 111–124.

Runte, R. (2001). Re-educating humankind: Globalizing the curriculum and teaching international ethics for the new century. *Higher Education in Europe, XXVI*(1), pp. 39–45.

Sachs, J. (2008). Improving global health in the developing world. *Brown Journal of World Affairs, XV*(I), pp. 115–119.

Saul, J. R. (2005). *The collapse of globalism and the reinvention of the world.* New York, NY: The Overlook Press.

Schaff, M. (1977). Marshall Plan. Retrieved on February 10, 2010, from http://web.ebscohost.com/ehost/delivery?vid.

Schori, P. (2005). Painful partnership: The United States, the European Union, and global governance. *Global Governance, 11*, pp. 273–280.

Schumacher, E. F. (1973). *Small is beautiful: As if people mattered.* (3rd ed.). New York: NY: Harper & Row Publishers Inc.

Schwab, C. (2004). Fact sheet: Poverty in South Africa. *Southern African Regional Poverty Network.* Retrieved on June 14, 2010, from http://www.sarpn.org/za/documents.

Scott, W. R. (2003). *Organizations: Rational, natural, and open systems.* (5th ed.). Upper Saddle River, NJ: Prentice-Hall.

Shewchuk, V. (2010). Organizational ecology: Intangible assets in play with today's enterprise. *Knowledge Management, 3*, pp. 1–14.

Sridharan, S. (2009). From subsistence marketplaces to sustainable marketplaces: A bottom-up perspective on the role of business in poverty alleviation. *Ivey Business Journal Online, 73*(2), pp. 1–11.

Stiglitz, J. E. (2002). *Globalization and its discontents.* (1st ed.). New York, NY: W. W. Norton & Company.

Stockbauer, B. (2008). The future role of the United Nations. Retrieved on September 5, 2008, from http://www.share-international.org/ARCHIVES/political/po_bsfuture.

Tubbs, S., & Jablokow, K. (2009). Leadership development and adaptation innovation theory. *The Business Review, Cambridge, 13*(1), pp. 53–59. Retrieved on October 14, 2009, from ABI/INFORM Global.

Uhlfelder, E., & Lima, A. (2005). Micro loans, solid returns. *Business Week, 3932*, pp. 100–102.

Ulrich, H. G. (2007). Political ethics and international order: Introductory remarks to an international ethical discourse. *Studies in Christian Ethics, 20*(1), pp. 5–12.

Usunier, J. C., & Lee, J. A. (2005). *Marketing across cultures.* (4th ed.). Essex, England: Pearson Education Limited.

Verme, P. (2010). A structural analysis of growth and poverty in the short-term. *The Journal of Developing Areas, 43*(2), pp. 1–21.

Viswanathan, M., & Sridharan, S. (2009). From subsistence marketplaces to sustainable marketplaces: A bottom-up perspective on the role of business in poverty alleviation. *Ivey Business Journal Online, 73*(2), pp. 1–11.

Volkert, J. (2006). European Union poverty assessment: A capability perspective. *Journal of Human Development, 7*(3), pp. 359–383.

Walonick, D. S. (1993). Organizational theory and behavior. Retrieved on May 11, 2010, from http://www.survey-software-solutions.com/walonick/organizational/theory.

Weber, H. (2004). Reconstituting the "Third World" poverty reduction and territoriality in the global politics of development. *Third World Quarterly, 25*(1), pp. 187–206.

Wilbur, C. K. (2001). Economics, power, and regulation of multinational corporations. *Journal of Economic Issues, III*(2).

Wilbur, K. (2001). *A theory of everything: An integral vision for business, politics, science and spirituality.* (1st ed.). Boston, MA: Shambhala Publications Inc.

Wong, C. K. (1995). Measuring Third World poverty by the international poverty line: The case of reform China. *Social Policy & Administration, 29*(3), pp. 189–203. Retrieved from EBSCO database.

Wood, S. (1998). Issues and agendas: Building "Europe": Culture, history and politics. *Journal of Historical Sociology, 11*(3), pp. 397–411.

Xu, Q., Chen, J., Xie, Z., Liu, J., Zheng, G., & Wang, Y. (2007). Total innovation management: A novel paradigm of innovation management in the 21st century. *Journal of Technology Transfer, 32*(1–2), pp. 9–25. Retrieved October 14, 2009, from ABI/INFORM Global.

Yunus, M. (2007). *Creating a world without poverty.* (1st ed.). New York, NY: Public Affairs.

External Link: Global Marshall Plan Initiative. (http://www.globalplan.org/index-eng.html).

Reference: Retrieved from http://en.wikipedia.org/w/index.php?title=Global-Marshall-Plan-Initiative&oldid.

Endnotes

Philosophy of history: doctrine of spiritual inevitability xxx)—this philosophy is based upon the Greek notion of "eternal recurrence" as formulated by Friedrich Nietzsche. It is also based upon the notion of reincarnation, whereby individual humanity must, through a series of lifetimes, come to realize a state of spiritual perfection, and once that stage is reached, man inevitably overcomes his own mortality and thus is freed from the cycle of birth and death. Also, within this sense, history is a history of suffering humanity by which individuals inevitably arrive at a new rebirth of spiritual perfected man; this ultimate state of spiritual perfection is most often attained at either the fifth, the sixth, or the seventh state of spiritual awakening. Eternal recurrence is based upon life recurring within a cycle, for example, as the seasons of human existence—winter, spring, summer and fall—only to repeat the whole process over and over. In a sense, man is a bit like Sisyphus in terms of having to repeat the cycle of life over and over; Sisyphus is condemned to rolling a stone up a mountaintop only to see it roll back down again and thus has to begin the entire process once again. However, spiritual man at least has hope and faith that he or she will inevitably reach a state of historical perfection, a point in time wherein historical existence is finally transcended, and at that point, history as we know it is now dead to the spiritually perfected individual.

The goal as well as the challenge for humanity has always been and is still in the present the elimination of suffering, whether it be global poverty, the environment, the global crisis of political and economic subjugation, and the continual search for a higher awareness in which humanity as a whole must reach perfection on a holistic basis. This, as well, would transform mankind, according to Ken Wilbur, into integral humanity. I would submit that, as Marx predicted, capitalism will inevitably self-destruct through either another or a symbolic "dictatorship of the proletariat." In essence, according to Maitreya, there will be a worldwide stock market crash, and/or this will be the signaling event leading to a system of world affairs governed in terms of democratic socialism or some type of participatory democracy— however, one in which local communities, whether on a grassroots level or regional level, will decide for themselves.

Some intellectual authorities believe that since capitalism during the postmodernist age and beyond appears to be at best a tool of modern corporatism and its leaders—that is, maintaining corporate wealth for their own selfish ends at the expense of not just the poor and middle class but also working-class America—a new type of social democracy (i.e., participatory democracy) is arising that will focus upon both working classes, poor-and middle-class America, at the expense of decadent capitalism or perhaps some type of arrangement between working-class socialism and working-class capitalism.

The operative word is *transcendence*. Just as in the case of the Biblical Hebrew and Christianity, wherein an ultimate purpose is gained through the course of events on an historical basis, for Maitreya, transcendence is achieved through spiritual perfection. Christ himself transcended the cross and thus Earth itself (in effect transcending to the fifth level of spiritual perfection) and thus not having to reincarnate on Earth again (unless he should choose to do so). Christ is the example of human transcendence by which Western civilization, in particular, considers its ultimate purpose. History has, in reality, no meaning since the world itself has no meaning since the only meaning that can be justified in terms of history is man himself; as Camus stated, man is the only creature to insist on having and procuring a meaning and thus, inevitably, transcendence.

Historical determinism is itself a series of cycles of natural law. However, at any moment in historical time, man may transcend history as in choosing through free will that eschatological moment in time and, in doing so, has reached that spiritual moment. However, it is important to note that one cannot have a valid philosophy of history, whether of a divine or of a scientific nature unless, at the same time, you have a profound sense of faith, a deeply religious or spiritual sense of faith that transcends the physical world. It is only through that type of faith that one can ultimately have a beginning and eschatological ending of history. Thus, history is bound up in the end by faith in a transcendent, spiritual end. Burkhardt is correct when he limits mankind's ability to describe the historical process, although Burkhardt does not challenge man's ability to transcend history through faith; he simply states that man is limited in his knowledge of a transcendent historical process.

One of the most important implications of this, according to Fr. Richard Rohr, is the notion that there is absolutely nothing, whether good or evil, neither the spiritual or material world, that is not crucial in man's understanding of the universe, and beyond that, "whether our wounds are caused by others or by our own mistakes, Julian of Norwich frames it all as grace," saying, "First the fall and then the recovery from the fall, and both are the mercy of God" (Julian of Norwich, Richard Rohr's Meditation, July 2015). Or in other words, mystics, in their acceptance and understanding of both love and suffering, "have emerged with compassion for the world and a learned capacity to recognize God within themselves, in others, and in all things" (Richard Rohr's Meditation, July 2015). In essence, perhaps the most important implication of this is that any kind of dualistic thought patterns (e.g., good versus evil) is an illusion, while the mystical spiritual world of God's transcendent universe is one of goodness and love agape (suffering conquered by the force of love). Or in other words, the shadow is just as important as the light; the material world is just as important as the spiritual world. Neither can live without the other. According to Rohr, they both belong together. If we had no sin, we would never experience salvation. This is one explanation for the problem of evil in the world. According to theosophy writers, anything that deviates from the whole or oneness implies that there will be evil.

John Ralston Saul's book *The Collapse of Globalism* emphasizes the decline of globalization, which appeared to peak in 1995. Although, the decline has continued through the early twenty-first century, it is still unclear as to what the future may bring. What appeared beginning around 1971, the economic drive, especially by larger Western countries such as the United States and the largest of nations within the European Union, has given way to the emerging developing world, such as India, China, South Africa, and other developed nations within the Middle East.

Stiglitz's (head of the WTO from 1997 onward) 2003 book, *Globalization and Its Discontents*, is deeply critical of the IMF as part of a larger problem in which the West (primarily the United States), in driving the globalization agenda, garners "a disproportionate share of the benefits at the expense of the developing world" (Stiglitz, p. 7). Stiglitz goes on to state that the "Western countries have pushed poor countries to eliminate trade barriers but kept up their own barriers, preventing developing countries from exporting their agricultural products and so depriving them of desperately needed export income" (Stiglitz, p. 6).

The origins of globalization implied that "civilization should be seen through economics and economics alone" (Saul, 2005, p. 7). However, after the 1997–98 Asian financial crisis, with Malaysia imposing capital controls, this proved to be successful, strengthening the confidence of such developing countries as China, India, Brazil, and South America. This emphasized the importance of the nation-state (i.e., nationalism), the pervasive legacy of colonialism and the ambition(s) of the developed world (Saul, 2005).

It would appear that the entire notion of globalization—or, as Saul identified, globalism—is a double-edged sword of both an upside as well as a downside. As Stiglitz (2003) pointed out, while the opening of international trade has helped many nations "grow far more quickly than they otherwise would have done" and given some nations greater "access to knowledge," the divide between the "haves and the have-nots has left increasing numbers in the Third World in dire poverty, living on less than a dollar a day and lacking any sense of economic stability" (pp. 5–6).

Although globalization has brought positive change to some developing nations, such as improved communication and the elimination of artificial barriers, Stiglitz (2003) points out, it has failed miserably in erasing poverty in many parts within the developing world. Stiglitz also points out that more people are living in poverty in 2003 than were in the 1990s, although world income has actually increased (2003).

E. F. Schumacher's (1973) book *Small is Beautiful* addressed the issue of poverty quite specifically, depicting centralized government versus decentralized government or bureaucratic large government versus local, state, and regional government. One of the main aspects of poverty control, according to Schumacher, is the notion of individuals living in the large cities versus citizens living in the rural areas. Schumacher makes the claim that unless developing countries are able to develop sustainability within rural areas, technology and technologists within the large cities will fail to reach their goals in terms of any attempt to reduce poverty. In addition, according to Schumacher, if those rural areas are essentially a wasteland of poverty, these poor people will begin moving to the larger cities believing that they will find jobs there; unfortunately, they may be only digging a deeper hole, forced to live in poverty-stricken slums, and there will certainly not be enough jobs to go around—if any jobs at all (Schumacher, 1973).

What Schumacher (1973) believes is essential is the development of intermediate technology in bypassing the big cities "and . . . directly concerned with the creation of an 'agro industrial structure' in the rural and small-town areas . . . In this connection, it is necessary to emphasize that the primary need is workplaces, literally millions of workplaces" (p. 183). However, Schumacher also points out that many of the populations stuck within a cycle of poverty will need some form of aid, including food, medicine, teachers, etc. that they may be transformed into healthier human beings and thus, in turn, ready to be taught in some form of intermediate technology if not on sustainable methods of agriculture.

What this writer needs to do is to, as Ken Wilbur addressed, "develop a theory of everything." Wilbur's sense of an interior and exterior consciousness implies something holistic in nature. All human beings are perhaps different in their ability to address both political and economic notions. We are all at a different level of existential or moral and spiritual development as well. According to Wilbur, who addressed all levels of development, from the first stage of tier one to the transcendence to tier-two thinking, all levels must be fully accepted for what they are, a chain of being that can only begin at the first step of ascension, and everyone must first address the initial issues of development to chronologically advance to higher levels until the stage of green is reached, the end of tier one and the beginning of advancing to second-tier thinking. To do this, we must also address the issues that are addressed in this book, beginning at stage-one awareness, again leading to tier-two awareness. Once people advance to tier-two awareness, a sense of the interdependence of humanity becomes one of the core issues. At this point, individualism is transcended, and individuals instead reach a point of organism rather than organization. At this point, issues such a global poverty and environment movement can be successfully confronted because individuals at that point have the mental ability to do so. Within this sense of Wilbur's notion of tier-two thought, it exemplifies when individuals are able to initiate into a higher level of spiritual consciousness. Thus, the belief that global poverty can be transcended in the near future, I would submit, is not possible until a greater level of humanity has transcended into tier-two thinking and, as a result, more people are becoming initiated into higher levels of consciousness. Maitreya cannot intervene with a miracle to accomplish this since he and the other masters cannot interfere in the free will of mankind. That is a sacred duty for all individuals involved in mankind.

What this writer/researcher is referring to is nothing less than a new paradigmatic shift of thinking, a change of attitudes, a focus upon cooperation within the global village rather than competition as being the main underlying motive of projected change. What we are talking about here is also nothing less than new ways of looking at society, particularly within the United States and the European Union, whose addiction to market forces is keeping them from focusing their energies into helping those suffering in poverty throughout the world, particularly throughout the Third World (where starvation is killing millions of people each year).

Just as the United States helped the German people in post-WWII society, that same initiative and sense of compassion that propelled the Marshall Plan forward could even, at a much greater potential level, not only help feed all the starving masses in the Third World as well as other parts of the globe but also provide enough medical supplies and doctors to eventually erase the scourge of rampant disease within these same global areas. Once again, a shift in paradigm from market forces and competition to one of cooperation is a new kind of politics in compassion that would work from a pragmatic perspective.

Obviously, the United States is nowhere near where it needs to be concerning this paradigmatic shift, but there are recent signals that, given the tenuous nature of the stock market, people are finally coming to a realization that simply relying upon the market forces of competition is not the final answer. In terms of achieving greater happiness, many people are finally (slowly but surely) realizing that focusing upon cooperation with other people—whether it be fellow neighbors, citizens, or peoples of other nations—will, in turn, provide a much greater and more lasting sense of security and satisfaction. On a political, social, and economic sphere, a focus upon democratic socialism, including participatory democracy, will provide the best underlying paradigm shift in terms of government structure not only in the United States but also in the EU and in cooperation with the UN; this will enable people throughout the world to begin to start sharing resources, and this again implies an emphasis upon a spirit of true cooperation. Within this perspective, Professor Mayor, former head of UNESCO, is especially enlightening. Professor Mayor (cited in Font, p. 3) concluded that to help Third World nations stricken with poverty and hunger and to prevent conflict, economic conditions need to be created that will allow poor nations to gain emancipation and self-esteem, and in turn, politicians must understand that the creation of peace involves the prevention of conflict and the promotion of "peace-building" (Font, p. 3).

The global Marshall Plan in rushing food and supplies to the Third World has actually already been accepted by all the nations of the world as well as by the WTO and the IMF (Muller & Stoger, 2009). However, the problem lies in the fact that although great plans are formulated on the world stage, nothing happens because funds are limited, and at present, the United States is focused almost entirely on homeland security (Muller & Stoger). My solution to this is if there is greater, much greater emphasis upon a Marshall Plan, thus alleviating much suffering and poverty, there would be much less violence on a global scale, and thus, the need for more funds for homeland security would not be needed. That is also the vision of Maitreya and the masters.

Either the EU, the United States, or the UN also cannot achieve global economic justice unless practical support is received by NGOs, the business sector, and society at large (Muller & Stoger, 2009). The basic recommendation challenging the EU, the United States, and the UN is to work together on a pragmatic scheme to finance and implement the Millennium Development Goals of the UN (Muller & Stoger). In doing this, plans can be put in place, again on a pragmatic basis, for eradicating extreme poverty and hunger, ensuring environmental sustainability and achieving universal primary education, along with the long-term perspective of an ecosocial market economy as a global political framework (Muller & Stoger). This is only a beginning, however.

Printed by Libri Plureos GmbH in Hamburg, Germany